How to Start Up & Manage Your
STAND-UP COMEDY
Career

By Barry Neal

©MMVI Magic Lamp Press
Venice, California

This is a work of fiction. Names, characters, places, and incidents are either the product of the author's imagination or are used fictitiously. Any resemblance to actual persons, living or dead is entirely intentional, or coincidental.

How to Start Up
& Manage Your
STAND-UP COMEDY
Career

ISBN: 1-882629-38-8

Stand-Up Comedy
Career Management

Section I
Introduction to Stand-up & Open Mikes

Section II
Finding Your Voice

Section III
Analyzing the Audience

Section IV
Performance/Surrounding/Stages

Section V
**Showcasing, Fee Negotiation, M.C.,
Booking Rooms and Getting Paid**

Available at bookstores, online
and also available as an eBook
http://www.comedyschoolvideos.com

Foreword

There has been no shortage of books written for aspiring stand-up comedians. Most of them are a series of interviews with successful comics, each giving some sage advice to the wannabees. Others just seem to fall into the self-aggrandizing category of "hear me toot my own horn, about how funny and popular I am."

Unfortunately, we were not aware of any attempt to let the non-professionals in on that real inside information that every comedian must know: how to manage a career. This is the backstage stuff that can make or break a career, because unlike the rules concerning many other jobs, just 'showing up' and being funny don't cut it. Those two are important, but they're only the tip of the career management iceberg. Sure, people like Paris Hilton or Kevin Federline reportedly can earn $25,000 just for showing up at a party, but a successful comedy career can last much longer if done correctly, and is much more immune to being destroyed by a few facial wrinkles or the passing of a 30th birthday.

Up to now, there has been no way to learn the 'unwritten' rules of professional conduct that a stand-up comedian should follow: the only way to learn them was by trial and error – the 'hard way.'

Barry Neal has been learning those rules for more than fifteen years now, and as a result of following what he considered to be the 'right' ones, his career has gotten off the ground quite nicely, leading him to appearances on the stages of comedy clubs throughout the country, appearing on the *Tonight Show,* and now a very busy career as a comedy coach, talent booker, and manager/rep for many other comedians and entertainers.

As owner of a production company, I became familiar with Barry's popular routine as the 'Counselor of Love,' and was impressed by the way he turned a 'clean' act into a profitable business.

It wasn't until meeting him that I discovered his reasoning. As he put it, the best way to get out of the comedy clubs and into the world of big-budget corporate gigs was to develop a routine that could be performed in front of executives and their families.

I also wasn't aware of the jobs being made available at corporate functions, but soon learned that that's where our former elected officials turn to make the big bucks after leaving office. Agencies like the Washington Speakers Bureau send out former presidents, sports figures, TV personalities, and others, for fees that reach up to $250,000, for a half-hour speech and a seat at the CEO's table... and if they can pay that much for the main speaker, they have no problem paying a measly five to ten grand for an opening act, like a 'clean' comedian.

If you have any intention of going into the entertainment profession by being a stand-up comedian or other performer in front of the public, you owe it to yourself to learn what Barry has found to be the 'rules' to follow.

We were fortunate enough to have caught Barry during a break in his busy schedule, when he had a few days off to sit down an put his thoughts into a 5-volume set of videos/DVDs containing over 100 areas of advice for the aspiring comedian: from the few basic elements of stand-up comedy, all the way to those all-important business aspects of booking jobs and getting paid.

He has allowed us to have those programs transcribed and presented in print, resulting in this book... the first of its kind, and the type that the most successful of them all, Jerry Seinfeld has often mentioned, as being needed.

Gene Grossman – Magic Lamp Press

1

Introduction

I've been doing stand-up comedy for about 17 years and have been teaching a class and doing seminars for about eleven. So, this is your first step on a long journey. I want to thank you for taking this first step. It's a long hard road but it's worth it.

Stand-up comedy has done great things for me, and this is what I love to do. I also love to teach, so again I thank you for making this book your reference for the management of your future comedy career.

And, keep in mind that Comedy is a Serious Business.

Barry Neal

2

<u>Focus and Hard Work</u>

We're going to really concentrate on two things here in this section. One is hard work. That is really the final arbiter on how successful you'll be. I wish there was a magic wand of stand-up comedy that can touch you on the head and say *you have so much talent, you now will be successful.* It simply doesn't work that way. So number one, you have to be willing to do hard work. And just by having this book you've already taken the first step, so congratulations.

The second thing we're going to focus on is having a plan – having a focus. There's an old saying, "If you fail to plan you plan to fail." I know it's corny, but it's true. If you don't have a focus, if you don't have a plan, you're not going to be successful at stand-up comedy. So, again those are the two things we're going to concentrate on and then, we're going to get into the whole world of stand-up comedy in terms of analyzing audiences, how to book a room, performance, surroundings, finding your voice and professionalism. But those two things are the key: having a plan and hard work.

3

A Little History

My background is really in comedy. I started doing stand-up when I was in college at Northwestern University, which is near Chicago. I started doing what were called *open mikes*. That's when clubs open up their doors to anyone who wants to do stand-up. I was only 19 years old back then and I thought it was a lot of fun. I stopped doing it for a few years and I got into what's called *improvisational comedy*. At Northwestern there was a thing called *The Meow Show* that a number of famous alums have done. It was a lot of fun and made me confident on stage that I could be funny. The director of our show who was actually the executive producer now of Drew Carey's *Who's Line is it Anyway?* took us to Europe and I also did acting when I was there and I thought that really was my passion. I'm going to be an actor. I'm going to be a comedic actor because I've done stand-up and I know how to do acting, so I'll move to Los Angeles.

Well, to make a long story short, if you move to Los Angeles without an invitation, without representation, you're going to be in casting calls with thousands of people and you're just another face. It was a long road and I realized I didn't think I really wanted to be an actor. I didn't really like doing Shakespeare. I didn't really like doing Chekhov plays. I wanted to make people laugh. Within six months, I knew I needed to get back to stand-up. At the time, there were still a lot of places that were doing open mikes. The IMPROV was one of them, so I went to an open mike and did really well. Maybe it was luck, maybe it was a good crowd, but for those five minutes I got people to laugh and I realized this is what I want to do. So I started going to every open mike I could: coffee houses, clubs, whoever would give me stage time, I would go and I'd write down my notes. These are the material that I'm going to cover this show. This is what I'm going to do the next show. And within six months, I thought I had 10 to 15 pretty solid minutes.

Soon I decided that I should go on the road, go to clubs, maybe start making some money, so I went on a road trip with a friend of mine and we hit all the towns near Los Angeles. We drove from LA to Phoenix to Albuquerque, to Colorado, Utah, Vegas and back home. We had a great time and I would showcase in these clubs. I would basically get up on their stage, do five minutes and out of the seven clubs that I did a showcase at, I got five clubs to hire me. And what that meant was, they liked what I did. So, like six months down the line they paid me to come back out and be what's called the Opening Act, the MC.

For someone who's 21, 22 years old, it was a thrill. I was actually getting paid to make people laugh. After a few years, I had a plan. I had a focus. I can't be the MC, the Opener anymore so my goal was to become the middle person, which is called the Feature Act. And in two years, I was able to acquire enough material, 30 to 40 minutes, to be a solid Feature Act. At that time, I also was at the Improv being an MC.

What I wanted to do there was learn from the best and I did. At that time, we're talking the late 80's, early 90's people like Seinfeld was there, Ellen Degeneres, Dennis Miller, and Bill Maher. Some of the best were at the Improv and I got to watch and it was exciting and I learned a lot. And then, I realized I can be a headliner. I just have to get a plan. So I watched them and realized what made them great and that is they were distinctive. They found their voice. And we'll talk about that in the later tape.

After a few years of featuring, I finally began headlining. And here's the interesting thing. I was headlining, I had my voice, I was doing pretty well, making decent money and I started getting TV shows. You'll see that I've done a couple "Evenings at the Improv's" and MTV, some stuff on Fox and other cable networks and what was interesting was when I did the MTV, David Spade was the host. I thought this is great. I'm on MTV. I'm young. I'm cool. I'm doing TV shows. My friends are going to call me. Nobody called me. Got one phone call. Not from a friend or family member but it was from Julie Brown's Production Company.

Julie Brown is a great comic actress and at the time she had a sketch comedy show and they brought me in, they liked what I did. Now, the show ended up going under but what was exciting is all of a sudden I was looked at as an actor. I got management out of it. I got an agent out of it. And I was going on these commercial auditions. And I kind of went through this whole circle of I wanted to be an actor when I first moved out, I found stand-up comedy

6

and it led me to being looked at as a comic actor because I was really good at what I did.

And point of fact, I really don't know much about acting and it was kind of funny, the first commercial that I did. I went in, no training and it was a laundry detergent and I'm working with this young girl and they say to me, "Give me your slate." I didn't know what they wanted. So, I'm like, "Nah, I don't even know what you're talking about." Well, they think I'm kidding, so they're laughing, thinking, oh, he's a comic, he's funny. Then, they said, "Who are you here with?" I look at the girl and I said, "Well, I'm here with her. She's kind a cute but I don't know her name." Now, they're just in hysterics thinking that I'm just a cut up.

The fact of the matter, I didn't know what a slate was. They just wanted to know what agency sent me. And they asked me, I told them the agency and the casting director actually went up to the girl who had probably 50 times more training than I did and said, "Just follow Barry's lead. It's a comedy spot. He'll know what to do." And I'm thinking, follow my lead. I don't even know what a slate is but that's how it all came full circle for me.

I started out wanting to be an actor. I fell into stand-up again and when you get good at it, we're going to talk about how the whole world opens up when you are really good at any one thing. And that's my background and now that I've done stand-up and now that I'm doing stand-up, I never want to leave. I may get a TV show. I may not but even if I do, I will always come back to stand-up because it is the most rewarding thing that I've ever had in my life

4

What is Stand-Up Comedy?

So, what is stand-up comedy? Now, that you know a little bit about me, a little bit about you, what is stand-up comedy? Well, here's what it is. Stand-up comedy is a dialogue. It is a dialogue between the performer and the audience. Repeat. It is a dialogue not a monologue. Some comedians are called limnologists. I don't like that term because again, stand-up is a dialogue between you and the audience.

Even though the audience may not verbally be saying anything out loud, they're speaking volumes. How are they speaking? Through their body gestures; they're sitting like there, looking around. They're telling you something. If they're laughing, their eyes are on you: they're telling you something. A lot of people take my class who are actors and they say, "Well, I'm going to do a comedy monologue for my show." It's not going to work. Why? Because the audience needs to feel as though you are talking with them.

9

There is an interaction. The audience needs to believe that by their laughter, their emotion, that they can move the show in a certain direction. Well, by definition of monologue, it is just that mono. It's one. You almost put up a fourth wall. You say, "I don't need the audience. My stuff is funny onto itself." That's fine, if you're doing a Shakespearian monologue for a casting director. It is <u>not</u> fine for stand-up. I've seen people do monologues. It never works. Because again, the audience starts feeling, "Wait a minute, it doesn't matter if we laugh, we don't laugh, we move in our chairs. This person has a set prepared material and he or she will not sway from it."

And if the audience feels you can't sway from your material, why should they care? The audience needs to feel like a part of that dialogue. Stand-up comedy is not about jokes. It's about giving of yourself. Talking to them. Again, jokes are not going to last simply because the audience will begin to say, "Wait a minute. They're just up there telling jokes. They're not really revealing themselves. We're not having a discussion. They're trying to make us laugh."

Comedy Career Management by Barry Neal

The magic of stand-up comedy is when someone is on stage and looks as though they're just saying funny things. "Hey, this happened the other day." Watch a stand-up. You'll always hear in their act, "You know I just went to the store the other day." Well, guess what? They didn't go to the store the other day. They went to the store five years ago when they wrote the joke. But the magic is making the audience believe that it's dialogue. That's why a lot of stand-ups actually are very good comic actors, because they're make believe there's that interaction. "This just happened. Oh, you know what? I was just outside and I saw this guy." I wasn't just outside. I didn't see that guy. I wrote this bit two years ago. But the audience believes it. I've made it so they feel as though there's this newness, this freshness. There's this spontaneity, and that's the magic of stand-up.

This is a very spontaneous art form. You're saying things like they've just happened. They're coming off the cuff of your mouth. "Hey, just...this is what I'm saying right now." And the audience reacts to that and there's that bouncing back and forth and that's where that relationship comes in. So, it is not about jokes. I will sometimes see a comic say, "Here's a joke you can take home." That may get a laugh because again, it's an old joke. It's been around for 50, 60 years, you know. Two guys walk into a bar, ba-da-bing.

However, you cannot do a series of jokes and think you are going to sustain laughter. Try it. Go up to an open mike and do like 10 joke jokes. By the tenth, the people are going to be like -- you're not giving of yourself. Stand-up comedy is giving of yourself and talking with an audience -- not just talking to them. People say, "Hey, tell me a joke." "I don't know any jokes. Actually, I think I know one joke." Here it is and it's a funny one but again, it's not giving of myself.

Guy's in a bar and there's this little piano player playing on a little piano. It's like 10 inches tall. He's playing beautifully and next to him is a magic lamp. Well, some patron walks in, goes up to the guy, and says, "That piano player is like 10 inches tall. He plays beautifully. Where did you find him?" The guy says, "Well, I found him in this magic lamp. This lamp can give you anything you want." The guy thinks about it. He says, "Well, how much will you sell it for?" The guy says, "$100,000." The guy thinks about it. Writes him a check right there for $100,000, takes the lamp, and thinks, "Ha, ha, what a sucker."

He rubs the lamp and says, "I wish I had a million bucks. I wish I had a million bucks." Boom! He looks around the bar. There's a million ducks. Not a million bucks. There's a million ducks. He goes up to the guy and says, "I asked for a million bucks, not a million ducks. What - is the genie deaf?" The guy says, "Yeah, what'd you think, I asked for a 10" inch pianist?"

It's an old joke. A funny joke but you do see how clearly I'm just doing a joke. There's nothing spontaneous about it. There's no real connection with the audience and that's what stand-up comedy is. It's a connection between you and the audience. It's a relationship. I'm going to talk more about that in a little bit. The other thing about stand-up comedy that we need to talk about is how it has to be interesting. So, when you start getting material, make sure it's interesting.

Remember the game, rock, paper, scissors? Rock crushes scissors. Scissors cuts paper. Paper covers rock. Interesting always beats funny. Okay? If you want funny, tell jokes. People will laugh for a little bit but they won't stick around. If it's interesting, they'll stick around for a long time. And we'll discuss that in another section. But again, when you're starting out, I'd rather have you be interesting than try to be funny because quite frankly, any good teacher can take something that's interesting and make it funny. That's the last step in stand-up comedy - when you're teaching.

If you give me something interesting, I can make it funny. But I cannot take something that is not interesting and maybe funny and make it interesting. People want to sit and watch interesting.

5

The 3 Elements of Stand-Up

W e're going to talk about the Three Elements of stand-up comedy. The first element is <u>material</u>. You have to have something to say before you even get up onto the stage. The material can be great, or it can even be so-so, but it should be something that you care about, something that you want to talk about. So, the first element is gathering material.

The second element is the most important: <u>delivery</u> of that material. So, delivery is element number two. And I'm going to give you a phrase. I'm going to say it now and we're going to say it over the course of these next couple sections, and you're going to be tired of hearing it, but it's really important. **It is not what you say but how you say it.** I'm going to say that again. It is not what you say but how you say it. That's what gets the audience to laugh. It's really not so much the material, but how you deliver that material.

That's what makes Jerry Seinfeld the best. He knows how to deliver the punch line. You can give a great comic average material and he'll know how to deliver it so it gets laughs. I guarantee you; you give a bad comic or someone who's not a comic, average material and throw them up on the stage. They will not know how to deliver the material. They will not get laughs. That will prove to you it is not the material. It is the delivery of that material.

Third element: <u>audience</u>. You need to have an audience for there to be a stand-up comedy show. There's an old adage that says, "The only difference between a crazy person and a stand-up is an audience." You know, that's true. If you don't have the audience there, who are you going to have a dialogue with? That's often why when you watch comedy on TV, you think "this isn't that funny." Why? Because you're not in the room. You're not part of the audience. You're at home. You're distant. There's a fourth wall. There are distractions. The microwave's happening. The kids are screaming. People are outside... whatever is happening in your house, you're not in that room.

If you've never been to a stand-up comedy show, go. It's a completely different experience than listening to it on tape or watching it on TV. There's an energy in the room that's hard to describe. But the energy is there because there's that relationship that we talked about between performer and audience. So you really need to be there.

Those are the three elements. <u>Material:</u> you need to have something to say. Two – <u>Delivery</u>: it's not what you say but how you say it, and third, you need an <u>Audience</u> that's there, and ready to laugh.

6

<u>Talk & Watch</u>

As you will learn from this book, I want to talk about certain subjects. One is *Talk & Watch* comedy. You've already taken the first step and you've purchased this book: you're trying to learn about stand-up. The best way to learn is through experience. Go to some club. Go to an open mike. Rent videos. Watch comics. Talk with other comics. Do it in a positive way. When I say *Talk & Watch* comedy, too many times people are like, "Hmm, I see this person and I'm funnier than they are."

Try to talk and watch with a positive attitude. The reason those people are on TV is not an accident. It's not some mystery. They're on for a reason. Try to figure out that reason. Now, you may not like them. You may not think they're funny, but in point of fact, someone thought they were good enough to put on TV. So, you're job is to figure out why. Talk and watch comedy. Learn.

One of my greatest experiences was when I was at the Improv being an MC.

Again, try to keep your mouth shut as much as possible and listen. You can't learn while your mouth is going. And that was really what I did. I just shut my mouth and I would get into conversations with some of the great comics. It was almost chilling because I looked up to these guys and I was in a conversation with Bill Maher, Larry Miller and Jerry Seinfeld. And I wasn't saying anything; I was just 22 or 23 and I'm like, wow, these guys are great, but I learned a lot.

I learned how they watched an audience and how they developed material, and it was fascinating. It's very important: if you want to get good at something, talk it and watch it. That's your job. Learn about it.

7

Attitude

When you hit the stage, you want to bring attitude. You don't have to fake an attitude. You don't have to fake being mad or fake being sarcastic, but you have to have an attitude, because again, you are giving off feelings and that's what people connect with. It's not what you say but how you say it. So, the feeling that you're giving off is what people are really concentrating on, and either agreeing with or disagreeing with, but they are connecting with you with feelings. Okay, we're going to talk about that in another segment but again, you have to have an attitude. Everyone has one.

I might say, "Well, my wife lost her car keys," or I could say, "Yeah, wife lost her car keys," or maybe, "My wife lost her car keys." That's saying the same thing three times but I said it with three different attitudes. One was kind of inquisitive; just, "She lost her car keys. That's strange." The other one was sarcastic. "Yeah, she lost her car keys. What a shock." Third one was just mad. "She lost her car keys. I can't believe it. I'm so pissed." Have an attitude. Okay?

20

When you get up on stage, people connect with that. Don't just get up there and talk, blah, blah, blah. People want to hear what you're feeling inside and the only way to express that is to get it out through your voice, through your gestures, have an attitude. You have to. Otherwise, people are just going to listen to a talking head. Hopefully, I'm not just a talking head because I'm excited. I'm excited to be here and hopefully you can get that from the energy that I'm giving. 'Cause otherwise I would just sit back and go, "Here is stand-up comedy. Lesson number one is this..." Who cares? If I'm not excited, how can you be excited? I love doing stand-up. That's my life. That's my career.

I want you to do stand-up comedy. I want you to enjoy some of the things I've enjoyed. So, again bring an attitude to the stage. As soon as you have that, people will connect with you.

8

A Stand-Up Doesn't Tell Jokes!

One of the things that I'm going to stress in this section as well as in the other sections is that we don't tell jokes. Stand-up comedy is not about telling jokes. Jokes are for the office. If you want to tell jokes, go to the office and say, "Hey, I got a funny joke." That's not what stand-up comedy is. I'm going to say something that's a little bit complicated but I'm going to say it twice so we all can get it. A stand-up does not say things so that he can tell jokes. A stand-up tells jokes so that he can say things. Sounds strange doesn't it? What did he just say? Well, I'll say it again: A stand-up does not say things so he can tell jokes. A stand-up tells jokes so that he can say things. What's the difference?

The difference is this. The end result is really not the joke. If you just want a laugh, you can get a laugh. I've seen bad comics literally pull their pants down, tell jokes, old jokes like bar jokes and they get laughs. They're not good comics. They don't go anywhere. So, the end result is not just about the laugh. The end result is about saying things... things that are important to you. Almost like having a theme that you're trying to discuss with the audience. Along the way, you have to tell jokes. You have to get them laughing but the end result is this thing that you want to discuss.

Now, this thing doesn't have to have a great social relevance. You don't have to be a great political commentator, although certainly Will Durst is one. You don't even have to be a Dennis Miller, who wants to say things about society. I think he's brilliant but you can be sophomoric. You can say things that are important to you that are silly.

Let's talk about Seinfeld. He talks about the Minutia, but it's important to him. So when he talks about being like Superman, or he talks about breakfast cereals, it's important to him and that's what you need to do. Don't worry about the jokes. Anybody can tell a joke, almost anybody. But not everyone can say things that are important and at the end of their set have people say, "I got a good feeling. I laughed and I learned something about them."

What you want to do is establish. You want to give a part of yourself. This is how I think. This is how I feel and give it to the audience. And that's how the audience connects with you. They understand what you're thinking. They understand what you're feeling and they agree with that. So, it's not just this fourth wall, "Hey, here's a joke. Go ahead and laugh. Don't worry about who's telling it." You're selling yourself up there, okay? So go ahead, give a part of yourself and say things. Yes, we're going to use jokes along the way, but ultimately we want to say something that's important, important to us and hopefully the audience will agree.

9

Know Your Victim

Stand-up comedy is not a victimless crime. There's a victim in every joke that you tell. Often the victim is you, and that's fine. Nobody's going to take umbrage at the fact, "Hey, you can't make fun of yourself." But sometimes audiences will take offense when a victim is not an appropriate target. If you're going to make fun of, say your grandmother, you'd better make sure she really deserves it, because audiences love grandmothers. If you're going to talk about your cat, make sure you're doing it in a way where the cat kind of deserves to get some punishment. I'll give you an example.

One of my comedy students came up to me with this joke. It was an old joke, but I didn't want to have to go into why it was an old joke because maybe he didn't know. And he actually told me it was a true story, which is another thing I want to mention. Never tell the audience "it's a true story." They don't care. Not only don't they care, but what are you telling them when you say, "Hey, this is a true story", what are you really saying? You know - the rest of the stuff, that's all BS. I made that up. So don't tell them "it's true." The audience believes pretty much what you say is true to some extent. They want to believe.

So the student comes up and says he takes this girl out on a blind date, takes her to a restaurant, the girl looks at the menu and she says, "I guess I'll have steak and lobster." And he says, "Well, guess again." He also told me he never got a laugh, and he said, "Why?" And I said, "Well, you're a jerk." I told him that the girl's not an appropriate target. You know, maybe she shouldn't be ordering steak and lobster on a blind date, but your, comment of "guess again" is just rude. I told him "One -- you're a good looking guy." And he was. "Two -- he was successful," which he talked about in his act; so all of a sudden this rich, successful, good-looking guy is telling some girl on a blind date to "guess again." Just rude. I said make her an appropriate target, and then we'll laugh.

He said, "How do we do that?" And I said, "Well, let's say you pick her up in your Mercedes and she said, "Oh, I thought you had a Rolls Royce. I guess this will be okay." And you go to a restaurant and she said, "Oh, I thought we were going to go to a better restaurant. I guess Spago will be okay." And then, you sit her down at a table, a nice table and, she said, "I thought we could get the head table. but I guess this will be okay."

Well, now the audience hates this girl. She's being a bitch. She deserves her comeuppance and we can't wait for you to get her. So, when she orders and says, "I guess I'll have steak and lobster." And I said, "Guess again," the audience might even applaud because we don't like this person. We don't like her. She's been rude to you and when you tell her to guess again, we applaud you because now you're kind of the underdog. Audiences root for underdogs. [Seabiscuit, Titans, Hoosiers]

Watch any *"National Lampoon"* movie. Watch any real comedy and who always wins in the end? It's almost always the underdog. So make sure when the underdog wins, they defeat the person who is clearly the favorite, because the audience will root against them. The big institutions, *National Lampoon* and *Stripes*, who's the underdog? Bill Murray. What the institution really is the butt of the joke? The US Army and Sergeant Holka by extension. So, again he gets to be the butt of the joke, because no one's going to stand up and say, "Wait a minute. I'm rooting for the US Army."

The US Army is a big institution. They can take a few hits. Think about *Animal House*. Who is the butt of the joke? The butt of the joke really is Faber College, and by extension, Greg Marmalard, that fraternity, you know, Neidermyier. They're really the butt of the joke. They're the victims but they're good victims because they're kind of evil. Who's the underdog? It's the Delta House with John Belushi. So when the Delta House defeats Faber College, defeats Vernon Wormer, and Marmalard, and Neidermyier, everyone cheers. They're happy. That's always the way it works.

Take *Revenge of the Nerds*. How many people do you think would have left that theater happy had the jocks beaten the nerds? Nobody. The nerds have to beat the jocks. So again, when you're doing stand-up, pick an appropriate target. If you're going to make fun of somebody, make sure that the audience agrees that they should be made fun of.

10

<u>Your Stage Persona</u>

I'd like to talk about persona. What is a persona? Persona is merely short for personality. Everyone has one. Find out what it is. Persona will also be synonymous with finding your voice. We're going to discuss that in depth in the next chapter. However, when we talk about persona, I want to mention that every persona is real. Even a one that's crafted and seems fake, there is some reality to it. I'll give you an example -- Andrew Dice Clay. There's a part of Andrew Clay Silverstein that is Andrew Dice Clay. What he does is take that part of him, magnifies it 100 times, and he comes up with that character Dice.

Pee Wee Herman is really Paul Reubens. There's a part of Paul Reubens that is Pee Wee and he just magnifies it and brings it out and shows it to an audience. And why were they successful with it? Because there's a part of all of us that is Pee Wee, that innocent child in all of us. As much as we don't like it, if we like Andrew Dice Clay, there is a part of us that likes that Andrew Dice Clay, that tough talking kind of misogynistic mean, New York tough guy. There's a part of you if you like Andrew Dice Clay that identifies with that.

Every persona, as fake as it may seem, is real. [Ask your parents about Jack Benny's stinginess] Here's where it comes into play. It's difficult to get rid of that persona. If you build your persona that way, it's very difficult to change. We're going to talk about that in a little bit but again, finding your persona is simply tapping into who you are and magnifying that for the people. There are different facets to us. We can't show all the facets.

Jerry Seinfeld has a personal life. Jerry Seinfeld has sworn in his life but in his act, it's not what he chooses to reveal. He chooses to reveal this side of his persona. You'll never know anything personal. He doesn't talk about his wife, and he doesn't get vulgar. But there's a part of him that is sexual. There's a part of him that is personal. He chooses not to talk about it, and that's okay.

Bill Cosby talks about family. I'm sure there's a part of Bill Cosby that is political. He has political views but he chooses not to show that. So, your persona is real but it's a part of who you are that you magnify 100 times. I go by the counselor of love. I talk relationships. I talk about men and women, specifically my wife and myself. There's a part of me that is very different from that, but I choose not to show it, and that's okay. I'm not saying that I'm a serial killer and that's the part I'm not showing. But on stage, I choose to show that one part of me and I magnify it 100 times. And that's really what you've got to do, tap into the part you want to talk about. Bring it to the stage. Magnify it and, that's your persona. That's your personality.

11

You Only Have One True Persona

You really only have one true persona. I know that we're revealing a part of ourselves and magnifying it but that should be the part of you that really takes over most of your life. When I say Jerry doesn't talk about things that are personal or I don't talk about things outside of my relationships, that's really what consumes pretty much my daily life. I talk about sports on stage because again, I'm very much a sports fanatic but it's the context of my relationship.

When you reveal that persona, it will be the thing that guides your career. We talked about Pee Wee Herman and Andrew Dice Clay. One of the things about revealing yourself is that once you reveal it, you can change and alter it a little bit because we change all through life, but it's difficult to say, "That was an old persona. I now want to do something completely different." So, you only had that one persona and you can get typecast. You know, a lot of times people have done *"Superman"*, whether it's Christopher Reeve or George Reeves the

32

original. They've been known to have said, "Wow, you know we really can't seem to get out of that role of always being thought of as "*Superman*"."

It's the same thing with stand-up comedy. If you build a career being Pee Wee Herman, it's very difficult to get out of that, because people will always see you as Pee Wee Herman. People will see you as Andrew Dice Clay. He's done different things being Andrew Silverstein, and now he's back to Andrew Dice Clay. And I'm not putting him down because he's a fantastic performer and he's made a lot of money and been very successful, but once you've revealed that persona to a mass audience and millions have seen you and know you as a certain type of person, that may be it for you. Do you think Jerry Seinfeld could become an Eddie Murphy and be really edgy and racy and talk about things political and be vulgar? There's no way. The audience would never accept it.

Jerry made his career by being clean and observational. He will go to his deathbed being clean and observational to the audience and that's great. He found his persona. He tapped into it. You have to be able to reveal yours. Once you do, you'll be successful. But until that point, you'll always be struggling. So find that part you want to tap into, get up on stage, reveal it, open it up, magnify it and you're on the road to being successful.

12

How Do You Know You're Funny?

Okay, now that we've talked about your persona, you're probably thinking, "I think I found my persona. How do I know if I'm funny?" Well, here's what I suggest. If you think you found your persona and you think you're funny, look in the mirror. Do your act. Are you laughing? Well, if you don't think you're funny, stop. That's pretty much the first clue. You haven't found your persona or you're not funny. But let's say you do your act in the mirror and you think you're hilarious. Try to find some objective, honest people. Not family members or friends, but objective honest people that think you're funny.

Okay, let's say you found some objective, honest people and you do your act and they don't think you're funny. Well, you've had one of two problems. One, you haven't found enough honest or objective people or two, you're not funny. So, in the end if you really feel you found your persona and yet nobody is allowing you on their stage and nobody is paying you, well, guess what? It's not a conspiracy of evil. It's your answer.

Comedy Career Management by Barry Neal

13

Open Mikes

Do you remember how I talked about hard work in the beginning and having a plan? If you fail to plan, you plan to fail. Here's how you get started in stand-up comedy. You're doing a lot of writing. You have your writing every day. And I don't care if you think it's funny or not funny but just get into that habit. Write every day. Give yourself an hour. Now, you have to go to open mikes. You have to try your material out. There's no point in having all these books with jokes if you don't have a stage or anything to present them on. You've got to go to open mikes.

Open Mikes are clubs, bars, coffee houses, and other public places that let performers go up, do their three, five, or seven minutes, and perform. Is the open mike experience fun? No, it's not. As a matter fact, in a word, it sucks. But you have to go through this process. Everybody does. Anyone who has had any success has gone through this process of developing their material and developing their persona by going to open mikes.

Why do these open mikes suck? Well, quite frankly, one -- if there is an audience, they're not expecting you to be that funny. So that's already a problem. Two -- there's so many comedy clubs out there, most objective honest people who just want to laugh go those clubs. They don't go to open mikes. This means you're going to be relegated to doing your material in front of people who are other comics or singers, and they're really just waiting their turn to get up on stage. It can be humiliating. It can be hurtful to your dignity. It can be a long arduous process and I wish there was something that I could say to help you avoid it. I wish I had that magic wand that would let me say, "You don't have to do open mikes" - but you do.

And again, there's no shame in saying, "You know what? I can't go through this. I don't have the time. I can't make the effort," but if you're one of those people who really want to do stand-up comedy, if it's in your heart, if it's in your gut and you want it more than anything, and if you're reading this book, I think you may be one of those people, and you'll have to go through the open mike experience.

It's best if you can find a buddy... someone that you identify with, that you feel as though they're strong and they're competent. Go together. Work together like a team. He watches you. You watch Him. And it's so much easier when you have a buddy who's also doing these open mikes, because otherwise you're there alone. You're there for hours. You're waiting in line. It stinks. At least if you have a buddy, you guys can make it through together.

So, try to keep a positive attitude. We talked about that. If you're gonna go do this, keep a positive attitude because it's not all fun and games and laughter. Okay? Keep positive. Go through the open mike experience. Learn. Learn every day.

14

<u>Complacency</u>

I'm going to talk about complacency. Maybe you've got 10 good minutes and you say, "Why should I write? The places I go up, they never give me more than 10 minutes." Well, because if you start getting complacent, it breeds arrogance. And no matter what your perceived status is in the stand-up comedy biz, if you get complacent, you're never going to get better. And the great ones always get better.

So, yeah, you may have 10 good minutes, but eventually someone may ask you to do 30 minutes. So take that 10 and get it to 15 and have a plan. By the end of the month, I'm going to have 20, then I'm going to have 25 and 30 and then, my plan is to take the 30 and cut it back down to 20 solid, great minutes. And, then I'm going to build it back up. A lot of times you think you have 30 minutes. Just because you can talk for 30 minutes doesn't mean it's 30 minutes of great comedy.

A lot of times young comics who have been doing it six months, say, "Yeah, I got about 45 minutes." I promise you, you don't have 45 minutes. It takes years to build up 45 rock solid minutes for you to be able to headline. So, yeah, be able to say I got 30 then break it back down and go, "Okay, these 20 kill." Then, build it back up. The great ones are never complacent. Woody Allen. Robin Williams. Steve Martin. They're always doing different things and that's what makes them great.

<u>Dare to fail</u>. There's nothing wrong with failing. The great ones have all failed. The only way to succeed is to fail first and then get better. Don't worry about having a joke not work. That's what the open mikes are for. It's okay. You go out, you risk it. You can never have great reward without great risk. Don't be complacent. I've seen comics get complacent. They're out of the business.

Even headliners -- I have seen one particular headliner who had 45 minutes: he toured the country, and always said, "My 45 minutes kill." And they did, but you know what? After he toured the country once and the audience had seen it, the next time they wanted to see it a little bit different. I'm not saying change all 45 minutes but it's got to be a little bit different, but he didn't. He did the same 45 again, went back a year later, again, went back another year, again. People stopped seeing him. There was nothing different. He got complacent and didn't write anymore. He got arrogant. He's out of the business.

The great ones never get complacent. If you want to be a great one, keep writing. Have a plan. Focus. Keep working hard. It's not easy. The great ones never take the easy road. They take the tough road and the tough road is writing every day, getting up there and even though you know you have a joke that kills, do a new joke. See how that goes. It's scary, but once again, the reward can be great.

15

<u>Always Be Prepared</u>

I'm going to say something that sounds like it's for only if you're a Boy Scout, but always be prepared. If you are not prepared to do stand-up comedy, don't do it. Now, I'm not saying you should venture into it by reading this book and running out to the nearest local club. Every time you get up on stage, be prepared. Don't get up on stage and start riffing because you feel as though you just want to talk and you didn't really prepare that day. That annoys me. That annoys every club owner. That annoys every comic. It is very difficult to get stage time especially in Los Angeles, New York, really in any city. So, what you want to do is you want to have a plan. If you fail to plan, you plan to fail.

When you get up on stage have a plan. Be prepared. Get up in the morning and say, "I'm going to work on these five minutes and I want to do these five minutes in a different way. I'm going to do the jokes and I'm going to look this way or I'm going to look that way, or maybe I'm going to be a little more low key. Maybe I'll talk to the audience on a certain joke. Maybe I'll try to use a different punch line." But be prepared. If you're not, you're wasting time. And I've seen a lot of comics do this and you will too.

When you start going to the open mikes, you'll see some people who have been there for a long time. They make the same mistakes. They get up on stage and start saying things like, "So, what else is in the news? What do you guys want to talk about?" Nobody wants to hear that. The audience is there sitting back, thinking, "We just want to hear what you have to say. We're tired. It's up to you, you...you're the one on stage. You tell us what you think. Don't ask us our opinion. I'm tired. I don't want to give my opinion. I want to listen to you."

And that's why you have to be prepared. That's why you have to do your work during the day and if you have a day job, during your break, you sit there, you write out your five minutes. Maybe a new five minutes, but figure out what you're going to do. Otherwise, you are wasting time, and stage time is precious. It's so valuable. There are 100 people behind you who want to get up on that stage and want to work stuff out. And if you're up there jerking around by saying, "Hey, what are you up to?" or, "Hey, you were here last week. I really liked your set. Hey, what about that new movie? I don't have a joke for it but boy was that movie bad?" You'll see this kind of stuff happen over and over. These are amateurs and they will always be amateurs. Don't do this. Be a professional. Have a plan. Be prepared and utilize that plan. The more focused you are, the more hard work you put into it. Remember those two things, and you will rise above that faster. You don't want to be in open mikes very long.

People who are in the open mike scene for any length of time usually tend to stay there, because they don't have those two things. They're not willing to work hard, and they don't have a plan. If you have those two things, you'll quickly get out of the open mike routine. You'll start working professionally. And all of a sudden, when you start working with professionals, you'll see the difference. You'll see audiences become better. You'll see the environment that you're working in become better. You're not working coffee houses. You're working clubs, and all that hard work will pay off. So again, hard work and planning for yourself, that's the way to go.

16

Three Types of Acts

When you start to make the rounds, you'll see that there are three types of acts in the usual stand-up comedy show, and they start out with an <u>Opener</u>, who almost always acts as the MC. He has to do 10 to 15 minutes. There is also a <u>Feature Act</u>, that's also sometimes referred to as the middle act. He has to do 30 minutes. Then, there is the <u>Headliner</u>, the closer, who has to do between 45 minutes and an hour. If you don't have that kind of time, you simply can't get out of the open mike scene. You'll be relegated to doing open mikes and coffee houses, until you can do 15 minutes, before you can even think about being on the road and working and getting paid.

So, again, you may have 15 minutes, but do you have 15 *solid* minutes? Because if it's just 15 minutes of talking, you don't have 15 minutes. So, as I've said, you must have that plan. That was the plan that I had when I started out. I wanted to be an opener so, I worked my routine up to be 15 minutes. Then, I thought I could be a feature but that would require 30 solid minutes. And when I finally got to the feature stage, I realized I needed more than 30 minutes, because what happens if you're the feature act and they say, "Oh, you know what, the headliner can't make it tonight. Can you headline?" What are you supposed to say? "No, I don't have 15 more minutes?" That's bad.

Or what if you have to stretch five more minutes? The boss might call out to you, "Instead of doing 30, hey do 35." If your answer is "Ah, I don't have 35," He'll never bring you back. So, if you're supposed to have 15, you better have at least 20 to 25 because there's always a chance of getting lost. If you forget some of your material, you can bring in other stuff. If you're supposed to have 30, you'd better have 45, just in case you have to stretch and headline. If you're a headliner and you need to do an hour, you better have an hour and half of material, because you may lose some material. You may say, "Oh, this relationship stuff's not working. I'll do the family stuff."

So, those are the three types of comics that will be on every bill. There'll be your opener. They open the show. It's a very tough spot. We'll get into that later on, but the opener has the toughest spot. The feature sometimes is the cushy spot. Why? Because you're following an act that probably hasn't done all that well and you only have to do 30 minutes.

So, you're following that. No one expects all that much from you and then the headliner, in my opinion is the easiest spot. Some people will disagree but I think it's the easiest because people expect you to be funny. You also have the most authority on stage and we'll get into that a little bit when dealing with hecklers. But at least those are the three types. The opener, The feature, and The headliner.

Have a plan. Give yourself two years to jump up from one level to the other. Give yourself two years before you're a solid opening act. Then go spend two years becoming a solid feature act. Then another two years to become a solid headliner. Most people don't headline before five years. It is very, very rare that you can actually do 45 minutes in a club and be a headliner. Have a plan and work hard. Be prepared. Every time you step up onto a stage, be prepared, and you'll find yourself getting away from that open mike. And then you may go back in a few years to that open mike and see a friend or whatever and you'll see those same people. It's almost sad in a way.

After five years I was headlining. I worked very, very hard. I was still featuring some clubs but I was headlining most of the clubs after five years, and the amazing thing is, I started teaching that. So, I'd go to these open mikes to recruit and some of the same people that I was doing open mikes with, they were there. And they're like, "Oh, we haven't seen you in a few years. Are you still doing the open mike?" It's kind of embarrassing to go, "Ah, well, no, I'm really teaching now. Headlining. I just did a couple of TV shows."

And all of them, they all had the same problem -- they didn't have a plan. They didn't take it seriously. Comedy is not a joke. I'm going to get to that in another section. So, again, hard work, be focused, and have a plan. Make a six-year plan to become headliner.

17

A Stepping-Stone?

Now, you may be purchasing this book and thinking, "I don't really want to do stand-up. I just want to learn how to do it well enough because I really want to act." Well, that's how I got started, and here I am, headlining all over the country. I've done TV shows too, and this is how I make my living. What I realized was that stand-up is not merely a stepping stone... it is an art form unto itself. If you want to act, if you want to be a musician, if you want to sing, go get books about that. This is a book for stand-up comedy.

Can it also be a stepping stone? Of course, but don't think of it like that. You have to be great at stand-up for that to launch your career in another direction. If you want to act, take an acting class. Don't think it's going to work like, "Hey, someone saw me and I was just average. I did five, six minutes and I'm decent on stage. Now, I'm in a sitcom." That's not how it works. You better be damn funny for people to look at you and say, "I want this person in a sitcom." No one's going to take you if you're just average, and the only way to get good is by hard work. It doesn't happen in two months. It doesn't happen in three or four months. It doesn't happen in a year. It takes years to get good, especially if you want your own sitcom.

Think of the people who have had the sitcoms. Center it around them. They're all ten-year veterans. Jerry Seinfeld, Paul Reiser, Ellen Degeneres, Paula Poundstone, Tim Allen, Drew Carey. These people have been doing it for years on the road. Ray Romano and Kevin James are great stand-ups. They've been dedicating their lives to stand-up. They became the best in their field and it was easy for them to launch, because they showed their persona, and it was really easy for them to transition it to TV.

Nobody gets a sitcom after just six months, because you don't have your persona yet. You don't have that ability. So don't think it's a stepping stone to being a comic actor. It is only if you're great, and you're only great if you dedicate yourself, you give yourself those years of hard work. Then, it can be a stepping stone. If you watch the commercials in between the sitcoms or in between any shows, you're going to see many stand-ups that you may or may not recognize. Why do stand-ups get commercials? Because they know how to deliver a punch line.

Can it be a stepping stone to being a commercial actor? Of course, but the ones that are making most of the commercials, were headliners. They weren't just average Joe at that...at the Ha, Ha Cafe. They were actually headliners. You don't know the names but guys like Scott Larose, Chip Chinnerie, Tom McTeig, all these guys put years into stand-up and they're still very good stand-ups. They're great stand-ups.

But first, they proved themselves in the stand-up circuit. They proved they know how to deliver a punch line, and just like the story I told you in the commercial audition where the casting director said to the girl, "Hey, follow Barry Neal...Barry Neal's lead, he knows what he's doing," these guys know what they're doing. That's why stand-ups make very good commercial actors because we know how to deliver a punch line.

You have 30 seconds. You better be funny. Stand-ups can do that. But again, they hire the best. They don't just look around at open mikes and go, "Oh, you're a stand-up? Come on in." You've got to be the best. Watch the sitcoms. Not only ones that star the comedians, but the...the secondary characters... Kathy Griffin, from *Suddenly Susan*. David Spade, from *Just Shoot Me*. There's one in almost every sitcom, and sometimes two characters that have been stand-ups. Why? Because stand-ups make good sitcom supporting roles. They know how to hit the joke, but remember, all of these supporting people are people who have done stand-up for awhile. They're the best at their craft. So don't look at it as it's just a quick stepping stone, like "I'm just doing this so I can get somewhere else." Do it focused, become the best - and then, all of a sudden you're career can open up.

I'll tell you a real quick story. I went to a Northwestern U. function (where I went to college) and Gary Marshall, another NW alum was there. He told me something that I'll never forget. He said, "Be like Colonel Sanders." I didn't understand what he was talking about. He said, "Do one thing great." I said, "Why?" He said, "If you do one thing great, you can run the industry. You can do anything in the business if you're great at one thing, if you're the best."

And that's true. Why did non-actors like Michael Jordan and Shaq get to make movies? Because they did basketball great.

Being from Chicago I might be biased, but I think Michael was the greatest of all time. So, why does he get to star in movies? Because he's Michael Jordan! That's why. Do they take average players? I don't think so. You don't see Will Perdue making movies. Now, I don't mean to rag on Will Perdue because he's a former Bull and I appreciate him for the championships he brought, but he doesn't make movies, because he's just an average player. People who are just average can't transition into other fields. Bon Jovi is now an actor. Why? Because he's a great rock star... and not a bad actor, either.

And it moves from field to field, great people in other fields move in a weave. I'll give you Gary Marshall as an example. He was a gag writer in the 50's on what was called Sid Caesar's *Your Show of Shows*. Sid had some of the best: Woody Allen, Mel Brooks, Gary Marshall. They were gag writers. So, what happened? Gary became one of the most well-known gag writers, and when he became the top of his field they gave him a show. It was called *The*

Odd Couple. He executive produced on that show, and then began producing more shows -- *Happy Days, Laverne and Shirley, Mork and Mindy,* and Gary Marshall wound up being the funny guy of ABC.

Now that he was running those TV shows, he got brought into movies, and they asked him to help with a dark comedy called *3000*. Gary helped: when he was through with it, it became a comedy-romance that did very nicely at the box office. You might even have heard of it... it starred Richard Gere and Julia Roberts. It was released as *Pretty Woman*... and it also featured several good comedic actors: guys like Jason Alexander and Larry Miller... and Gary Marshall.

Gary Marshall is in movies. Do you think Gary Marshall gets into that because he's a great actor? I personally think he is a pretty good actor, but he gets in because he's making these TV shows, he's making these movies, so, it's easy for him to go, "Hey, I'd like a role in that." Who's going to turn him down? And he was great in *Soap Dish.* He was great in *Lost in America* playing...playing the casino boss. And don't forget his continuing role as head of the network in the long-running TV show *Murphy Brown.*

My point is this: don't think of stand-up just as a stepping stone to something else. Sure, it can launch your career in other directions. I'm not saying it can't, but you've got to focus. You've got to do the hard work. You've got to dedicate yourself for years to be the best, and when you become the best, the world opens up.

I may get a TV show, or I may not, but I want to keep getting better. I want to keep striving, having a plan and moving up in this world in stand-up. And then, if I get a TV show, great. So, again, use stand-up for what it is. It's an art form. Be the best, and I guarantee all those people that have TV shows, they will always do stand-up because once you get involved and once you stop thinking of it as a launching pad to something else, you realize it's the best art form out there. It's the most rewarding one out there. Jay Leno works a couple of evenings each month in a Redondo Beach, CA club, trying out new material – and he's not the only one. Jerry Seinfeld has returned to the stand-up circuit too, and we all know that neither of those guys is doing it because he needs the money.

So, go ahead read this book, study with teachers, and learn. Get *good* at stand-up, then get *great* at stand-up, and then go ahead and start acting, because I guarantee you, you'll come back.

18

<u>Release Fear</u>

Before we end this Section, I want to give you another piece of advice. I know I've said a lot of things so far, and maybe you'll want to go over and re-read some of them. We've talked about <u>having a plan</u>. We've talked about <u>hard work</u> and <u>focus</u>, what will make you a great stand-up, and what made me as good as I may be now, and hopefully, will keep getting me better. But nothing happened until I learned one thing: <u>Releasing my fear</u>. It is very scary being up on that stage. Why? Because you're up there by yourself. You are up there in front of an audience trying to make them laugh. When you release the fear of not getting laughs, that's when you can become a real stand-up.

When most people start out, they're like, "Oh, I want the audience to laugh so bad." Believe me the audience senses it. And when they sense you're nervous and that you want their approval, they'll withhold it. Then I finally said, "You know what? I don't care anymore if they laugh. I think I'm funny, and I think this routine is funny." Audiences sensed my confidence. They felt that confidence and they had confidence in me and I became a better stand-up. I would start doing jokes that I never dared do before because I thought, "Oh, it's too personal." Or "Oh, it's too weird." It was a silly one, but I used to do this bit: I would say, "I don't think I can marry my wife until she knows the answer to this question. 'What do 20 and 50 minutes past the hour mean to you?' It took a while, but when she finally looked me in the eye and said, 'Is that time for CNN Headline Sports?' I said Let's go to the altar."

You may not understand what that means, and you may. I would say 20 percent of the audience knew what that meant. When we got married in '93, at the time there weren't scrolls on ESPN of constant scores. The only way to get updates was 20 and 50 minutes past the hour on CNN, and it was very important to me that I always got my updates for baseball and football, and my wife hated it because she knew whenever I changed the channel, it was probably 20 or 50 minutes past the hour. So that joke was very personal to me and I thought not enough people are going to get it. But you know what? Enough people did - and it got a laugh. And it was exciting.

I finally was released of that fear and it set me free. It let me talk about anything. All of a sudden I was talking about things I never dreamed to talk about because I thought, "Oh, people are going to think I'm strange, or people aren't going to like me." Who cares? I am who I am. And that's why comedy's a little like therapy. You release that fear. You finally show who you are, and go, "You know what? Accept me for who I am, or don't accept me. I don't give a damn anymore."

When you have that confidence, the audience senses it. They think, "Wow, this guy's confident. I like this person." Audiences want confident people and that's what's exciting. You release that fear and it sets you free. All those chains that you have, they're gone.

I' like to end this first section with almost what we started with. Once you release that fear and you say what you want to say, it's very important to remember, it's not what you are saying but how you are saying it. You're saying it with confidence.

There are four more sections in this book, so please read on.

SECTION II: FINDING YOUR VOICE

1

<u>Introduction</u>

This Section is going to be about Finding Your Voice and Professionalism. And again, when we say finding your voice, it's finding your comedy voice – helping to tap into your persona. Persona, of course, being short for personality. These two things are going to be very important in getting you work – finding your voice, finding out who you are on stage, tapping into that, being able to communicate that, and then being a professional.

This is what separates the people who work, from the people who don't. You have to act like a professional and you have to look like a professional.

2

What Makes You Funny

First, you have to find your persona. You really have to think about what you want to talk about on stage What part of you do you want to show and magnify to the audience? To find that out, the first thing you should ask is, "What makes me funny?" People are funny in different ways. I have a lot of energy. I get excited. I'm a very expressive person – sometimes too much so in my personal life. My wife always tells me, "You know, you wear your emotion on your sleeve. Even when you don't say anything, you just emote how you're feeling." And a lot of times when I'm playing co-ed softball and don't want to say anything because I don't want to look like a jerk, my wife says, "You know what? Just by the way you're standing, everyone knows you're pissed." That's the way I am. I'm expressive. Some people are very quiet and sullen and they say little things on the sly. That's fine. Find out what makes you funny and use that.

The second part to finding your voice is figuring out what you want to talk about. That's simple: what interests you? Too many young comics think, "Well, what does the audience want to find funny?" You know what? Audiences don't know what they want to listen to. They just want to hear funny. It's often like casting directors or agents going, "I don't know who I want to pick. Hmm, I'll know it when I see it." It's the same thing with audience members. They'll know what's funny when they hear it. So talk about things that interest you. Why? Because if it's interesting to you, all you have to do is communicate why it's interesting to you, and it will become interesting to them.

We've talked about how Interesting is better than Funny. So again, if it's your interest, it's real easy to make it funny. So sit back, relax, and just say, "What do I think about?" If you're a sports fanatic, talk about sports. Talk about the minutia of sports. Talk about the betting lines, or some strange gambler you know. It doesn't matter. If it interests you, it's easy to communicate.

Some people think, "Well, what if I'm interested in astronomy?" It doesn't matter.

That's the beauty of it. The audiences don't have to really understand what you're talking about but they have to understand the feelings. Remember we talked about how we communicate? We communicate through feelings, and if you're excited and you're interested, the audience will sense that and they will go along with the ride.

I don't care if you like literature and you want to talk about Flaubert and Madame Bovary. Hey, terrific. Go with it. I don't have to have read the book, I'll just see through your excitement and the way you express that excitement. I'll be able to follow the story. So go with what interests you, and be committed to the routine. Be enthusiastic. And again, find that inner voice by just saying, "What makes me funny? How do I express the way I think and the way I feel?" Do that, and you're off to a great start.

3

Think of a Party

When we do stand-up, we're meeting new friends, so think of it as a big party and you're the one who just happens to be standing up and telling the story. You have the microphone, so to speak, at the party. And sometimes we all do that. Have you ever been to a party where there are five or six people standing around and someone says, "Oh, I have a great vacation story blah, blah, blah, blah, blah" and that kind of goes around in a circle, and sometimes you've got the microphone. You've got the audience and you go, "Oh well, when I went to Peru here's what happened. We lost the luggage," and you exaggerate a little bit of the story because you know you've told the story enough times, so you kind of know where the laughs are.

That's what stand-up is. It's a big party. Granted, you're doing all the talking for the 30 or 40 minutes, but it's a party. We want to listen to people who are interesting. Interesting beats funny. Again, go to the party. You see a guy with a lampshade on his head running around acting like a fool. He's funny, but for how long? Maybe for Five minutes, tops. After that first five minutes, the lampshade on his head grows tiresome and becomes a little bit annoying. Why? Because that guy is analogous to the person on stage just telling jokes. He's not really giving a part of himself. He's putting a lampshade on his head running around just acting like a clown.

A stand-up comedian is <u>not</u> a clown. It's a person giving a part of himself. Go to that same party and look for the interesting person. Think about the person that tells that great story. He may be an electrician but he's telling great stories like, "Oh, I had to go to this house and I almost burned the house down because I crossed the wires," and he's so enthusiastic. He's so excited about telling the story. He is someone you can listen to for hours. How long are you going to watch that jerk with the lampshade on his head running around? You'll laugh for two minutes and then after awhile you'll be like, "I'm bored with that" because there's nothing new. There's nothing really interesting. Interesting beats funny. Think of stand-up as a party. Get up there. Say things that you like to talk about that are interesting to you, and have an attitude.

Again, if it's interesting to you, you'll have an attitude. You'll have a take on it. You'll show your exasperation. "Ah, I can't believe I made such a stupid mistake at that electronic meeting. You know I went to the meeting and I almost flubbed up the whole interview." You'll be exasperated. You'll have attitude, or you'll be mad. "I went to the bank and I opened up the door for a guy, and this actually happened to me." Never say that on stage but I want to tell you this is actually a true story. I opened up the door, guy walks into the bank. He gets in line in front of me. I'm thinking, "Hey, I beat you to the door. I opened it for you. That's not fair," but I didn't say anything. I figured, "Alright, I'm being a gentleman." He gets in line in front of me. He goes to the teller. I go to another teller. He gets out just before I do. He drops his deposit slip. So before he leaves I go, "Excuse me sir. Your deposit slip." I give it to him. He walks out of the door. I'm five feet behind him. He just doesn't even open the door for me. Door slams right in my face. I just want to go, "You know what? I take back every nice thing I ever did for you, you little creep."

Notice I'm telling that story with attitude, because I'm mad. I'm mad at that person. So get up there, have attitude. And it doesn't always have to be anger. It could be again, exasperation. It could be shame, or embarrassment. It could be any number of things. But have attitude, because that expresses feelings. Don't just think, feel. Audiences communicate through feelings. That's how humans communicate.

Think about it. Go visit a friend. If she's telling you a sad story and just saying it in a very blasé way, like "So, I lost my job. My husband's leaving. My kid is sick," and she's very blasé, you'll be like, "Gee, that's too bad," because you're just saying words. You're not feeling, because wasn't emoting any feelings.

Now imagine her telling you the same story, but this time she starts to sob and says, "My husband is leaving me and I don't know what I'm going to do. My child is sick and I don't know where I can turn." When she starts with those feelings and the tears come, we feel like crying too. Have you ever noticed that? When someone is crying in front of you, you feel like joining in with

72

them. And when someone onstage in front of you is happy, then you're happy too.

That's how humans communicate. We fee, because we all have the same feelings – But we don't all think the same because we don't all have the same experiences. But we all have the same feelings. We all understand happy. We all understand sadness and anger and angst. So that's why people who are happy are good to be around because if they're happy, we're happy. If someone's enthusiastic, we get enthusiastic. That's why you must have that attitude, because when you have attitude, people will identify with it, and that's how humans communicate – through feelings. Don't just think up on stage. Don't just talk – feel.

4

Style, Delivery & Physicality

Part of finding your persona is finding what style of comedy you do, and there are as many different styles out there as there are comics. Some people like to do long stories. Others prefer one-liners. Some work are more blue, and others are clean. There's no right or wrong style, but find a style that you're comfortable with. And again, think of it as a party. Think of it as if you're on stage, and instead of 600 or 60 people in the audience, there are only six, and you're just telling a story that you've told a million times, because it's a fun story. That's kind of your style.

The delivery is very important. Again, it is not what you say, but how you say it. I know you're thinking, "I've heard it. I've heard it." I want that embedded in your mind. It is not what you say, but how you say it. That is everything.

Think about how you deliver a joke. Some people deliver a joke and they're manic. They just talk very fast and they're delivering the punch line and they're going and going and going. Others are more laconic. They take their time. They let you think about every word and then they hit you in the end with a quiet little zinger.

So again, think about that delivery. And then you also have to think about physicality. Physicality is very important in stand-up comedy. For me, physicality aids my jokes. For most comics, it will be a visual aid. I like being physical. I like to use my hands, my face, my eyes. It's all part of what I show the audience.

In a perfect world the audience would sit there very politely, relax, have a cup of club soda, listen to your jokes and think, "Well, he is brilliant. I laugh and I adore him." It's not like that in the real world. A lot of time they're a little drunk. They're tired from a long day at work. They don't really concentrate 100%. It's just the nature of the beast. Maybe they're thinking about their babysitter. They're thinking about the fight they had with their boyfriend or girlfriend. They're not thinking about you.

So I like to use visualize aids and my physicality to aid the joke. It helps because now they don't just hear the joke, they see

75

the joke. I'll give you an example. I used to do a bit about how my wife is one of those types of people -- she'll actually let the gas tank needle hit "E" then say, "Twenty more miles, what do you think?" And I'd say, "I don't know. Is this a game with prizes? Let's just get some gas."

That always got a laugh, but then I decided I'm going to be more physical. I'm not going to just say it. I'm also going to show it. Think about that. Don't just say things. Show us. Don't say that your dad looks for the remote. Show us your dad looking for the remote. Look around. Look. Be physical. Is it in my face? In my pants? Is it under me? Is it in my shirt? Show it. It's a lot funnier, because now you're not just saying it, you're taking us to the place where it's actually happening, showing your dad looking for the remote. "Where's my remote? In my nose? In my head? Where is it? I don't know." That's what's funny.

I did that gas tank joke with my wife and showed physicality and see if you notice a difference. I said, "My wife -- she's one of those types of people who'll actually let the gas tank needle hit E and then go, 'Twenty more miles, what do you think?'" I'm like, "I don't know. Is this a game? Are there prizes?" I'd act panicky – maybe a little frantic. "I'm scared... Please, let's get some gas." It's a lot funnier, trust me. I've done it thousands of times.

That joke now will get an applause break most of the time or at least a very big laugh. Why? Because I'm not just saying she's pinning the needle on E and I'm scared. I'm showing it. I'm taking you into our car, having her drive the wheel, using my hand as the gas tank needle, pinning it on E and having her go, "Twenty more miles". And then maniacally going, "What do ya think, ha, ha, ha, ha, ha?"

And then my reaction, I want you to show it. I'm not just going to say that I'm scared I'm going to show you. "I don't know. Is this a game? Are there prizes? Just get gas!" Makes a big difference. There's some attitude in that joke. There's physicality in that joke. Now that joke works for me. That's my style.

If you don't have that style, it's okay. There are some styles where you don't want to be physical. There is no right or wrong, but you have to figure out what your style is. If your style is all about the word, if it's all verbal, there really should be no physicality. Dennis Miller puts his hands in his pockets and just talks because you really need to concentrate on what Dennis Miller is saying. You should actually have a thesaurus with you because sometimes it can be a little complicated.

I'm so thrilled when I get a few of his references, but he's not actually showing any part of a story. He's just saying things that you need to concentrate on. It's almost like being in school. You must concentrate.

It's the same with Steven Wright, who does very ethereal stuff. Talking about having a life-size map of the United States in his car -- sure is a lot of trouble putting it in his glove compartment. Well, you've got to think about it. If it's a life-size map, you can't put it in the glove compartment.

The point is, you don't need to be physical if you don' want to. You can to let the people think. There are a number of comics that work like that. They just work all verbally and that's fine. They can be brilliant, but you don't want all those wild gestures to confuse the audience because everything that is important is verbal. There's still attitude but it's all verbal. They don't need the physicality to aid them. And maybe I use physicality because the jokes aren't that great, because my verbal wit isn't perfect. But for me, my physicality works.

Bottom line: if you are going to go physical, go all the way. Use your arms, your eyes, your nose – everything. You know the microphone. Everything can be used to aid your joke. So if you're going to go physical, go physical. Go all the way. Commit to the joke. If you don't want to go physical, keep the microphone in the stand. Don't let anything confuse the audience. Let them just listen.

5

What to Wear

Once you've found your style, or you think you've found your style, try not to switch it up. I know again there are different facets of our personality but again, you want to take the one that's most important to you - or at least the one you want to show to the audience, put it out there and magnify it. I worked with a student who would do Richard Lewis-esque material. He was frantic. He'd put his hand on his face and he'd go around and he was frantic. It was very funny although it was Richard Lewis-esque, but like 20 minutes into a set, he'd start doing Rodney Dangerfield one-liners and it was just very jarred.

Again, you really have that one persona. Don't change in the middle. People expect one thing and if all of a sudden you're changing, they won't know exactly who you are. They'll feel like there's a dishonesty. So once you've found your style, stick with it. Don't switch styles.

I also want to talk about something that is very odd for a man to talk about, but it's clothing. I am color blind. My wife actually puts clothes together for me. I don't mix and match clothes very well. However, it is very important what you are wearing. And you're probably saying, "Why? What difference does it make? It's really all about how funny I am. I'm committed to the joke." Well, think about the party. Why do we go over to meet some people and not meet others? You could say, "Well, because they're cute." Let's say you see a cute girl but she's wearing a t-shirt that says "I'm with stupid." Do you still really want to meet that person? Probably not.

When you get up on stage, people are going to judge you. People will judge you before you say word one. Before you grab the microphone, they'll be judging you simply by how you look. You probably think that's shallow, but it's true. So what you're wearing is very important. Think about what you want to wear, because it will represent who you are.

I wear a suit and tie, because I'm billed as the *Counselor of Love*. I want to look professional. I'm not saying that's right for everybody, but it's right for me. It fits who I am. Offstage, I'm never in a suit and tie; as a matter of fact, my wife always complains I'm always wearing too many sports t-shirts. But on stage you'll never see me without a suit and tie.

Think about what you're saying on stage, who you are, what your persona, your personality is, and go with it. If you want to wear a t-shirt and maybe short jeans, what you're saying to people is that you're young. You're going to be doing kind of hip stuff. You're probably not going to play Vegas. That's okay. You can't be who you can't be, so again, think about what you're wearing, how it represents who you are, and it should say something about you.

If you're not sure, and of course early on you're probably not, it's always better to dress comfortably but look professional. I have actually gotten rebooked at clubs by what I was wearing. I was at a club in Seattle where I still play. First time I had ever played the club, the club owner did not see my show the whole week. He wasn't there the whole week. He finally came in after the show Sunday night. I had gotten in his car. He took me to dinner. He drove me back to the hotel and he said, "I'm definitely going to have you back." I said, "Oh, that's great. I'd love to come back. I had a great time." And he said, "Do you want to know why?" I assumed he heard I had done a great job, until he said, "I heard you were okay, but I like the way you look." He added, "You dress professionally, and I like that. I can't stand when comics come into my club, people are paying $10-15 a seat and they see some person in a t-shirt. Makes it look like they don't give a damn." He goes "And you're in a suit and tie and I like that."

I was kind of taken aback, but that solidified my thoughts of always wearing a suit and tie because again, it makes it look like you're professional. I'm on stage. If I have a suit and tie, it gives me a little more authority, certainly as the Counselor of Love. So think about what you're wearing. If you're going to look unprofessional it may hurt you in the long run.

Now I'd like to give some advice to the women readers – the comediennes. I'm not Mr. Blackwell making fun of what people wear, but I'll tell you this: for women, what you wear is 10 times more important, because the audience will be looking very closely. Here's the problem. If you're a good looking girl with a nice figure and you come out wearing something that is rather revealing or it shows off your cleavage, you've got a big problem.

And why is that? Because usually, half of the audience is women. How do you think they're going to respond when they see a girl not only take a microphone in their hands, because all of a sudden you're a star and they're just sitting next to their boyfriend; you've got a microphone and you're also pretty? They're not going to like it. I'll tell you that right now. Pretty women have trouble in comedy if they're going to be too revealing.

Think about that. The women aren't going to like you if you're showing off too much, and the men are going to like you, but they're not going to be concentrating on what you're saying or doing; they're going to be concentrating on one thing -- maybe two things.

So, do you want to reveal too much? Not unless that's part of your persona and you want to be the sex kitten and play up the sexuality, and you're kind of making fun of yourself by being too overtly sexual. It worked for Jenny McCarthy and Rhonda

Shear, who were both in *Playboy.* They play off their sexuality, looks, and body, and that's fine, but don't go up there and just be oblivious that you look really good. Get some mileage out of it too.

On the other hand, I'm not saying dress drab or put a housecoat on, but I am saying just be very cognizant that what you are wearing will speak volumes, so as you enter that stage and grab that microphone, guys are going to be staring at you and women are going to be judging you. I think all you women know that women judge women very harshly. So, again, be very careful. Pick your clothes out carefully and again, be professional and if you're not sure, just look like a pro.

6

Limiting Styles

There are certain styles of comedy that will limit your career choices. I'm not saying you shouldn't do them, I'm simply letting you know that they will limit the amount of choices that you have in your career path.

One style that can definitely be very limiting is if you work blue. If you're not familiar with that term, blue means you work dirty. You have a lot of "f" words and the "s" words, a lot of words that can't be on TV - and the reason that it's limiting is for that very reason. You're not going to do network TV saying a lot of dirty stuff, or if the content is overtly sexual. You can't do a lot of TV appearances and quite frankly, that's where you're going to get some major national exposure. So please keep in mind the fact that if you're going to work blue, other than a cable special, you're probably not going to be on TV.

Using blue material will also limit the amount of places you can work. When you work for corporations, and there's a lot of money in corporate events, they almost always want a squeaky clean show. I'm able to do that because I can work an hour very clean. If you're going to be working blue, they can't hire you because again, it's corporate. There are families that are going to be there. They must have clean acts. Even a lot of stand-up comedy clubs now will prefer the few acts that go on before the headliner be clean for the simple reason that if a show starts out blue, it's tough to dig out of that hole. As a headliner, I almost always will ask the booking agent if I can either bring somebody clean with me who can feature, or if he can put somebody in there who is not too dirty.

I don't want to have to follow someone who's doing a lot of "f" jokes or a lot of vulgar jokes or a lot of sex jokes. I don't want to have to follow that. It puts the audience in a certain mind frame and it's tough to dig out of that.

One time I actually had to follow a guy in Detroit who used the "f" word 54 times in his act. People walked out during his set before, as the headliner, I even went on. The problem was that the only people who stayed were the ones who liked that kind of talk. I don't talk like that. And the show really suffered, so bear that in mind. If you work really blue, you're going to have a lot of trouble working many clubs.

Other styles that are limiting are if you work with props, because if you work with props, you really aren't able to show off your persona. How do you show off your personality if all you're doing is really jokes? And that's all props are. Every time you bring up a prop, it's like here's something that's funny. I'm going to say something funny about this prop. Throw it out. Here's something about this prop. You throw it out. It's a series of joke, joke, joke, joke. There's really no flow. Each joke stands on its own and it's either funny or it's not, and you move on. The problem is the person doing these props has no persona.

Now you're probably going to say, "What about Carrot Top?" Carrot Top's the best. He's the best prop guy around. He makes a ton of money. He has a very successful career. So unless you're better than Carrot Top at being a prop act, you'll always be a second banana. In stand-up, you can be your own unique voice. There is no one great stand-up. There are hundreds up them because everyone has a different point of view, a different perspective. If prop you say prop comic, you think of only one person... Carrot Top. So unless you think you can be better than Carrot Top, you'll always be a second banana.

The other one that's also limiting is being a ventriloquist. The problem with ventriloquism is again, who's the funny one? It's not the straight person. It's the dummy. The dummy's the one that's funny. So again, you have really no persona if you're the one holding the dummy. Can you be successful? Of course you can, but it is limiting in where your career choices can go because all ventriloquists basically do the same thing. They all have a dummy, that is, a smart-alec dummy. Some of them have little cartoon puppets. The best that I know is Jeff Dunham and Peanut, a very good ventriloquist, but unless you're better than Jeff Dunham and Peanut, you'll always just be a ventriloquist who isn't as good as Jeff Dunham and Peanut. So again, it's very difficult because you have no persona when you're doing props or ventriloquism. It's really just someone or something else is the funny one... the prop or the dummy. Not you.

Comedy Career Management by **Barry Neal**

What's really interesting is I've worked with Jeff Dunham who is a great guy and very funny. What's funny is that the audience actually interacts with the dummy. The dummies have more of a personality than the straight man. I have seen an audience member get mad at a dummy because the dummy is going, "Hey, your wife is really cute. I'd like to haunt those." And the guy's like, "Hey, hey. That's my wife you're talking to." And he's getting mad. He's yelling at the dummy, and you sit there and go, "Hey, guess what? It's not the dummy who's talking," but that's what happens with ventriloquists and that's why it's very tough to have a lot of career choices. That's why you don't see a lot of ventriloquists with their own TV shows, because they really have no persona unto themselves.

The last style that's very limiting is what's called being a *hack*. A hack in our business, whether it's stand-up or any sort of art form, is somebody who does things that have been done before. They tread on the same topics. They steal material. It is the worst thing you can do, and I'll be discussing that next.

So again, certain styles can be limiting. If you work blue, if you work with props or a ventriloquist or if you're a hack, it limits your career choices. That's why I think stand-up comedy oftentimes is the best choice, because it's just you. It's your voice and with you, there's only one. You can go in a myriad of directions.

7

Hacks

A hack is someone who steals material, or does tired topics over and over again, somebody who has no original thoughts. Some hack topics, in general, if you're thinking about doing stand-up are things that have been done so often, who cares. "Hey, the east coast is different than the west coast." If you're thinking about doing that, stop, because again, these aren't important to you. These are just generic things that we all know. Or, "Hey, dogs are different from cats." Really?

If you're doing impressions that are really generic, like Jack Nicholson or Jim Ignatowski, stop. They're not funny anymore. I've seen hundreds of guys do it. I've seen women do Nicholson. I've seen bald guys do Nicholson. It's pathetic. Stop it.

Don't talk about airline food. Don't talk about commercials. "Hey, you ever notice this crazy commercial?" Yeah, we all have. The problem is that if you're doing stuff about commercials, too many comics are doing the same joke. If you're doing *Gilligan's Island*, "Hey, how come the Howells brought all that money?" I don't know. Who cares? I've heard a million comics do that. "Hey, how come the professor could build everything but a boat?" I don't know. Who cares? What's the point? You're not giving anything of yourself. You're not really being truthful.

You might ask, "but what if another comic does my same joke?" Well, if you're a hack, that's a problem. However, if you are true to yourself and you have your own voice, you can actually tread on similar material. You can actually have the same joke. But if you have your own voice, you're not stealing the material. You're not a hack. So, by definition, don't just change a joke because someone else has something that's similar because again, if you are true and you're doing it from your voice and your attitude, it'll get a different response because it's not what we say, but how we say it. Want proof? See *The Aristocrats*.

There, I've said it again and I'll say it again later on in this Section, and the next Section. It's not what you say but how you say it. Give you an example. Two of my favorite comics have the same joke, Paula Poundstone and Paul Reiser. It was literally the same joke. I'm sure they didn't steal it from each other, but it was in the news. But the way they did it, they came with a different approach so it's almost like a completely different joke. Paula did it on *Saturday Night Live*. Paul Reiser did it on TV; I think it was *The Tonight Show* and then later in his special. The joke is this, and I'll do it my way first just parroting it. Then I'll try to show it to you Paul Reiser's way.

Basically, the joke says that Sirhan Sirhan went up for parole. He went to the parole board and said, "You know if Bobby Kennedy were alive, I think he would give me parole." And then the joke is, "Well what a coincidence. The one guy that would give you parole and you shot him." It's a good joke. Now clearly, that's something that was in the news that a great comic could probably think of on their own but Paul and Paula came from different angles. Paul is more, "Wow, how does that happen?" He goes, "Ya' know, Sirhan Sirhan went up for parole and uhh..." (because he has a little Seinfeld in him if you listen) "he went up for parole and he said, 'You know if Bobby Kennedy were alive he would give me parole.'" And, I'm thinking, "What a coincidence. The one guy that would give you parole and you shot him. What are the odds of that? That's one in a million. Who knew?"

Watch Paul Reiser. He's one of my favorites. He's the "who knew" guy. Everything to him is, "How does that happen? I don't know. There's a guy. Who knows? That's how it happens. That's why." And that's why that joke is funny to him. He's like, "Well, what a coincidence. Bobby Kennedy would have given you parole and you shot Bobby Kennedy. That's weird."

Paula comes from a very different angle. She's much more thought provoking, much more inquisitive, I guess, in her tone. She goes, "Wow, Sirhan Sirhan went up for parole. He told the parole board he thinks Bobby Kennedy would have given him parole. Too bad. The one guy that would have given you parole and you shot him." They're saying the same things, very different approach, very different attitudes. People are going to laugh at each of them for different reasons.

Don't worry about someone having a similar joke. Again, it's how you approach it. And again, if you're unique, you're not going to have that many similar jokes. But again, if you're a hack, it's the worst thing you could be.

Here's another example: If you're a hack, you're never going to get work in this business. I worked with a guy in Florida. First time I had ever done a full week gig. I was getting paid, and the headliner that week was stealing, just stealing Kevin Pollack's bit. Kevin is a great impressionist, and he would always close by doing an Enterprise bit. He's on the Enterprise with Captain Kirk and he does William Shatner beautifully and then he does -- at the time it was original -- he was doing Jim Ignatowski from *Taxi*, because this was 20 years ago. He was doing Jim Ignatowski. He was doing Jack Nicholson as Spock and Bones and it was brilliant. Well, the guy I was working with, the headliner, was doing the bit almost verbatim. He had the Enterprise t-shirt and he was doing Captain Kirk, William Shatner, and he was doing Jim Ignatowski as Spock and he was doing Nicholson as Bones and I'm just thinking, "He's stealing this bit" but it killed every night. He would close and the audience went nuts, "Woo, it was brilliant!" and we became friends and I said to him I said,

"Hey, you gotta know that's Kevin Pollack's bit." And he said, "Nah, you know what? The audience doesn't care because they love it. And the club owners, they love me because the audiences love me." I'm thinking, "Wow, that doesn't seem right so the audience loves you and the club owners don't care so you're just going to steal a bit. Whatever. You're the headliner. I'm just a feature."

Well, a few years later we were booked together again. We did a show. I thought, "You know what? I'll do a show, a showcase here in L.A. I'll invite him because he's a friend of mine." I invited a girl. I thought, "We'll have a nice show. We'll do 10 minutes of comedy each stand-up and then we'll do some sketches." Well, we had a lot of agents and managers come to that show and one of the agents said to me, when the guy who was stealing the Enterprise bit was on stage, he said, "Oh, I didn't know he was on the show. I saw the flyer. I actually saw the girl. I'm interested in representing her. If he had been on the show and I had known it, I wouldn't have come." I said, "Why? Why would you not come just because he's on the show?" And he said, "You know why? Because he's a hack and if you're associated with a hack, then by definition you're a hack. It's guilt by association." And I thought, "Oh my goodness." I never did another show with this guy.

And as I talked with my comic friends who were beginning to be headliners and stuff they all said the same thing about the guy, "Yeah, he's a headliner but he's a hack." He got no respect. How are you going to get work in this town? You get work by your peers. That's how you get work. You have to have the respect of your peers. If you don't have that, you're never going to get ahead. This hack who was headlining, is now out of the business, because he had no respect. He never got good management, never got good agency representation, and never had the respect of his peers. So being a hack is the most dangerous thing you can ever become.

Don't sell yourself out just because you want to get a cheap laugh. If you want a cheap laugh you can get it. You can do an old joke. I guarantee it. If you do a *Gilligan's Island* joke well, you'll get a laugh. You do a Jack Nicholson impression decently, you're going to get a laugh. But don't sell yourself out. That's the road to the devil. That's the easy path. Don't do it.

Take the tough road. Get material of your own. Work through it. Believe me, it may take longer but it's a journey well spent.

8

Truth is Funny

Truth actually is funny. Does it literally have to be true? No, of course not. Do you want to preface a joke by saying this is true? No. Again, by prefacing that the joke is true, you're really saying that the rest of your routine is <u>not</u> true. Audiences sense when you are saying something that is truthful. That there's a germ in there that somehow started with the truth and although you're exaggerating a little bit, they don't care because they're involved in your story.

Here's an example of a joke that didn't work. A guy started out with his wife is so smart, yeah she was invited to join Menza, and he went on with this joke blah blah blah blah blah his wife is smart. The whole time I'm just going: this joke is not going to work because if he was telling the truth, he would at least be smart enough to know it's Mensa, and not Menza. Now that sounds pretty ticky tack. Well, that's really getting pretty harsh but you know what? The audience sensed it too. They sensed he was not telling the truth. The truth cannot be faked. Audiences are a little bit like children. They inherently know when you're telling the truth and again, the truth can be funny. You ever tell stories that are truthful? Sometimes they're the best stories. They happen in real life and sometimes they're so silly, you almost think that it has to be the truth. How could you possibly make that up?

Now again, we exaggerate a little bit. A lot of things that I say in my act, they started off as a truth. Are they literally what happened? No, not really. I tweak it. I take out stuff that doesn't need to be in there, that doesn't get laughs and it ends up being partially made up but it almost always starts with the truth because it's the truth for me. It's where it generates from. It generates from a true story, a true start. And then fiction, a little bit of fiction goes in just to add to the story.

Here's a joke I have that started off as true and I've tweaked it a little bit: My wife and I each have a car that we drive. I happen to drive a Grand Cherokee. It's a man's car. It could be a woman's car but it's my car. It's my man's car. My wife has a Miata. It's great. Pretty blonde girl in a

Comedy Career Management by Barry Neal

Miata -- terrific. I can't drive it. Let's face it. I'm about 6"1", 200 pounds. I'm in a Miata; people are going to question my sexuality. Well, my wife needed the big Cherokee one day, so I'm driving around town in the little Miata, going to a business meeting. I'm thinking, "All right, I know I look stupid in this Miata but I'm just going to drive and not look at anybody." I'm driving. This guy in a pickup truck is blasting music and he pulls up next to me. He's like some 22-year-old kid and I'm thinking, "Just don't look at him. I know I look stupid." But what was funny is that he's blasting music that's soft rock and I'm thinking, "You know, it's one thing if he's blasting heavy metal. He's blasting soft rock so I'm kind of looking at him and go you're kind of weird too." And I kind of give him a look just to see why he's blasting soft rock and our eyes met. Men are like dogs: whenever we meet eyes, it becomes a physical confrontation. So I kind of look at him and then kind of give him a guy look like 'whatever' and I look back, and he looks down at me and just goes, "Homo." I'm shocked. I'm thinking, "You know, I may look like a homo in this Miata but at least I'm not blasting Hall and Oates, so I think in the gay-off you lose."

Now that joke always gets a laugh. Did the story literally happen like that? No, it didn't. But you know what? It started with a truth, I was in the Miata, and a pickup truck did pull up. From that point I exaggerate a little bit just to tweak it and make it funnier. And now that joke works, because it started with the truth and people understand. I show them that story of me in the Miata going, "Oh no" and they understand that there's a truth and they believe that story probably did happen like that - or they just don't care. Sometimes stories can be literally true, but again, if it doesn't sound like the truth, people aren't going to buy it. Truth is funny and it can't be faked. Even children know what the truth is.

9

<u>Interesting is Better than Funny</u>

Earlier in this book, when talking about gathering material, I mentioned that *interesting* is better than *funny*. Here's a classic example of a superstar now, who is interesting, more than she is funny. If you don't know who Janeane Garofalo is, quite frankly I'm surprised you're actually reading this book. Janeane Garofalo was a stand-up in New York, and came out to L.A. roughly the same time that I was beginning to host at The Improv. She would do her material and not get many laughs at all. And I would sit and watch and to be honest, it wasn't my cup of tea, but she was doing something interesting.

She was one of the forbearers of what's now called *alternative comedy*, and basically it was this: She's not trying to get laughs; she's telling stories - and if they get laughs, terrific; if not, fine. She's just saying things, telling stories. There are no punch lines... she's just doing it. And she did it with attitude. You want to talk about selling stuff with attitude? Watch Janeane

Garofalo or David Spade. They're the fore-bearers of alternative comedy.

Getting on with the story, she was in L.A. and not getting many laughs at all and I would say out of the 15 people that would go up on stage that night, she got the least amount of laughs, easily, every time she would go up. Yet, within six months, she had two TV shows. She was on the *Larry Sanders Show*, one of the most respected shows on TV, and she was on the *Ben Stiller Show*, really one of the best sketch comedy shows, maybe ever.

How does someone do that? She's a very talented comic actress, but how does someone go from being a stand-up who's not getting many laughs, to getting on two television shows? The answer is that she was interesting. She was really different, and that's why she became successful. People would literally call me up, friends of mine, and say, "Hey when's Janeane Garofalo going to be on at The Improv? I can't wait to see her!" And I'm thinking, "Are you crazy"? Because I don't think she's that funny." But you know what? She had a following. She was interesting, and she was different.

Comedy Career Management by **Barry Neal**

Now here's my point: when you're interesting and different, people are going to notice. They're going to step up and go, "This person's doing something different." They may not like it, but they'll respect it. I respect what Janeane did. I may not have liked it, but I respect it. More importantly, some people are going to love it.

In a room with 100 people, she would rather have had 10 people love her and 90 people be apathetic, then have 90 people like her, and she's absolutely right. I really learned a lot by watching her and people who are doing alternative comedy. Believe me, anyone can be funny if you're doing stand-up a while, but you're only going to be successful if people love you.

I think about macaroni and cheese. I don't know too many people who don't like macaroni and cheese. Everybody kind of goes, "I like macaroni and cheese." But there aren't so many people that go, "I love macaroni and cheese. It's my favorite meal! When I go out to a nice dinner, I get macaroni and cheese." It's not going to happen, so don't be macaroni and cheese up there. Be different. Take a stand. Be unique. And don't ever be afraid to fail. It's okay. Janeane failed all the time, but with that great risk came great reward.

If you're different, people will notice. She definitely was, and she got a following going. And now there may be hundreds of thousands, who will watch Janeane in every one of her movies. She has a distinct persona, her personality. She found her comedy voice. She was different enough. She found a following. You will find it too. Be yourself. Let the audience come to you. Most of the other comics at The Improv were pandering to the crowd. They were saying, "I just want to get laughs. Give me your laughter," and that's easy. If you're a good comic, you can get laughter. What is hard is being yourself and saying, "I am going to stick to my guns. This is who I am. This is truth for me. You have to come to me." Because a lot of people won't. But you know what? That's the risk-reward. So go up there. Be yourself. Dare to be different. It'll pay off in the end.

10

Jokes Don't Last

If you're up there just doing jokes, they're not going to last. Again, think about doing knock-knock jokes, two guys walk into a bar jokes. First of all, they can be stolen rather easily. Even if you're doing it in your own voice, you hate to see jokes being stolen from you. My point is this. If you're telling stories, if you're doing things that are unique to you, you're telling from your voice, and nobody can steal who you are. So even if they take your joke, they can't steal the way you deliver it, the feeling that you're giving. Remember we talked about how people communicate through feelings? There's a relationship between the audience and you. You're relating through feelings. Someone may take my joke, but you'll never do my material as well as I can because it's me. I'm selling me.

Comics are sales people. That's all we are. We have a bag of tricks that we take along on the road. We open it up. We give it to the people. We're sales people. What are we really selling? It's not the jokes. Jokes come and go. People will watch my set for an hour, and come back and they'll remember maybe two of my bits. Here's an experiment for you to try: after you're done with this book, watch a DVD of a comic, listen to Jay Leno's monologue, listen to a comedy CD. How many of their bits do you remember the next day? One, maybe two, maybe three. When you listen to 45 minutes, what did you leave with? You left with the feeling that they gave you. That's what people communicate. That's how humans communicate – feelings.

Once again, it's not what you say, but how you say it, because those are the feelings that we communicate with. Nobody remembers my jokes. Like I said, there's maybe one or two because I consistently call them back throughout the course of my act, so the audience leaves remembering two of my bits. I don't mind, because all I know is afterwards when they thank me or I get emails saying how great the show was, it's a feeling that I give. My show is very positive, very uplifting and that's what I want to leave them with. Jokes don't last, so don't worry about the jokes. Worry about the feeling that you're giving people because that's what will last.

11

Getting an Agent

Young comics often think, "I want to get an agent to help me. I need an agent. They can help me find my persona." That's not how it works. You're putting the cart before the horse. It's really all up to you. It's incumbent upon *you* to put the hard work and the effort and the focus into it, so you find your persona - and the agent will find you, not vice versa. The agent doesn't say, "I think there's something funny about you. I'm going to help you find your persona." They don't have that kind of time. That's not their job. Their job is to take a finished product that they can make money off of. Again, in a utopian paradise, somebody would swoop up and take you and cradle you and say, "I'm going to make a star out of you, kid." That's not how it works in the real world.

The way it really works is, you put all the hard work in and you're ready to go, because you've put the five years in. You've found your persona. You have your voice. You have your material. You have your attitude, and *then* an agent comes in and says, "I can sell you. I can sell this on a TV show. I can make you a sitcom star or a second banana on a sitcom." That's what happens. You have to find your persona first and, that's when the agents come. It's a small world in the comedy business. Everyone knows who everyone else is, so don't worry about finding an agent or finding a manager. They're not going to help you, because you can't make money yet. If you're doing it a year, why is a manager taking you on? Agents and managers are in the business of making money. They're not the creative people. No offense if you're an agent reading this right now, but the agent is there to represent their clients. You have to be the creative one. You're the stand-up. You have to make your career choices. Show the part that you're going to show and then when an agent says, "That's what I like. I can sell that." Then they swoop in and take you.

Did I say "swoop in" like they're a vulture? Oops, I didn't mean that, but that's how it works. Agents will help you out when they feel they can make money off you. That's their job.

12

<u>Remove Your Mask</u>

We've already discussed ways for you to find your persona. The final thing you must do to get your persona out there is to remove your mask. You may be thinking "What mask? I'm not wearing a mask." Wrong. We all have masks that we wear when meeting new people. Think of that relationship: it's you and the audience. You're meeting a whole bunch of new people. Audiences come out because they want to meet new friends.

When you meet a new friend for the first time, you say hello, you shake hands, and you're wearing your mask, because your guard is up – all of your autonomic defense mechanisms. *I don't want you to get too close to me because I don't know you well enough.* You can't do that. We don't have time. Maybe you can give yourself months for a budding friendship, to slowly open up and reveal how you think and feel, and all these things. You have months, years to develop friendships. But with an audience, you just have minutes, so you

112

have to open up and reveal your masks and be vulnerable. You have to be vulnerable so when they don't laugh, it hurts, because you're revealing who you are.

You have to lower all of your defense mechanisms and say, "This is who I am. It's okay. If you don't want to laugh, that's okay, but I'm being honest with you. I'm being vulnerable." Audiences respect that. If you can't reveal your mask, then you have that fourth wall up and you're never truly letting them in to see who you are. And if you're never letting them in, then you'll never have that reward of having them laugh at who you are.

Think about your good friends. Friends that you've had for years can hurt you. Why? Because they know exactly what buttons to press. They know things about you that could hurt you. Conversely, you know things about them that can hurt them, but you don't do it out of mutual respect, and that's what makes the friendship great. That's what makes a great friend. I trust my friends. I have opened myself up to them and they know how to hurt me. Vice versa, I know how to hurt them. I don't do that. That's what makes a great friendship and that's why you love your close friends. Well, it's the same thing with an audience. You open up. You reveal that mask. You say, "This is who I am" and if the audience doesn't agree with you, it hurts.

That's why stand-up sometimes is the most daunting of all tasks, because you're on a high wire, and as much joy as I get from making people laugh and having people applaud, it's me that they love. It's that affirmation that I get, and that's great; however, I'm on the high wire. I'm like one of the Flying Wallendas (a famous old-time circus act). I don't have a safety net, and it can be very painful. It's like a knife in the heart when you open up and they just sit there without laughing, because they're letting you know that "We don't like you. We don't agree with how you think." And there's no one else to blame but yourself.

That's the weird thing about stand-up, but it's also the great thing. It's all you. You're the hero or you're the goat. An actor can say, "the director was terrible," or the script, stunk." But as a stand-up, it's all you. You're the hero or you're the goat and that's what makes stand-up different from all other art forms. You are live. You're in person, and you're letting 100 people into your world right away and they either give you that affirmation by going, "Yes. You are so on. We absolutely agree with you and we like you. We are your friend," or they go, "No. We don't like you. We don't accept you." And there's no denying that hurts.

You can't start crying on stage, but I guarantee you, if you do this long enough, there will be times you leave that stage and go home be close to being in tears; but you've got to work through that because not everyone is going to like you. Why? Because you're trying to be different. Yeah, you can be macaroni and cheese and you can have most people like you, but what's great is you have to be yourself, and you're being different, and not everyone's going to like you and that's that. As you get older, that's one of the things you learn. It's okay if people don't like me. I am who I am and I'm comfortable with that.

Reveal your mask. Show people who you are. It's okay. Some people aren't going to like you, but you know what? You'll like yourself for being able to confidently release your fears of not getting laughs and not getting loved, and showing it all to the audience. And believe me, the reward will be great because there will be people who will say, "You know what? You are my new friend."

13

It Takes 100 Shows

Now that you've found your comedy voice, I'd like to tell you the unwritten rules about being professional. First, before you judge yourself too harshly, you must give yourself 100 shows before you even think about judging yourself. Tape your first show. Tape your hundredth show. See where you're at, but don't get down on yourself. It's a hard process. Go through that process. Give yourself 100 legitimate shows and then start going, "Ahh, on that 94th, that wasn't a very good show." Then you can maybe get it down right because at least you have a year of experience behind you.

In terms of being a professional, the Number One rule is <u>always be early</u>. Now you may ask yourself, what's early? Well, if you are a 9 to 5 person and you get there at 8:57, you're early or at least you're on time. That's not the case in comedy. If you have a spot at 9:00 and you get there at 8:57, you're late. Better than that, you're fired. "But why? I got there early?" Well the point is you only got there three minutes before you're supposed to go on stage. People are panicking, going, "This person is supposed to be on in three minutes. If they're not in the room, what's going to happen?" Because there are several other acts that may have to follow, who can't just stretch their routines out because you're not there.

When I was MC at The Improv, this happened a lot, and there were always comics hanging around. So if I said, "Look, so and so is supposed to be here at 8:50 and it's 8:40 right now; this person who's on stage is going to end in five minutes. I'll do a few minutes in between, but I can't bring up someone if I don't know if they're in the room or not." And Mr. Friedman (Bud Friedman the owner), would usually say, "Find somebody else." And I would just call out to one of the other comics there, "Yo, do you want to go..." I'd know who they are. They're great comics. "You're not scheduled to go up. You want to go up and do so-and-so's time?" They would fill in and maybe finally, the scheduled person would get there at 8:57, but you know what? Mister not-on-time is fired. He's not working that night.

Get there early. Just by getting there early, they'll know you're there. Be on time. I like to get there about 30 minutes before showtime for a couple of reasons. One, I like to watch the comics that go on before me. I feel as though if you watch the comics that go on before you, you kind of know the feel of the room. You've already introduced yourself to the emcee. Now I can sit back and relax for a few minutes, and they can relax knowing I'm there. So, the number one rule, be early. It's always better than being late.

14

Being Polite

The second most important rule about professionalism, and this is going to sound so fundamental you're going to go, "I can't even listen to this part," but please do. <u>Be polite</u>. Now I know that sounds silly, but there a lot of people who are really bitter. If you're just starting out and you're already bitter, that's not good, because stand-up comedy should be fun. Yes, it's a business. Yes, I take it seriously. This is how I've made my life. This is how I bought my house and I'm going to send my kids to college, so yes it's serious, but it should be fun. Don't be bitter. Be polite.

Why should you be polite? One, it's the right thing to do, and two, you never know who you're pissing off. Develop good phone skills. What I can't stand is when people with no phone skill call me up. I book rooms, and that's one of the reasons that I think this book is going to help you, because I'm can give you not only the point of view of the comic, but also the point of view of the booker.

So when people call me up and they just go, "Hi I'm looking at doing some of your rooms." Slow the horse down. Try to ask me politely. I'm not saying you have to suck up, but these bookers, they get a lot of calls from comics. Be polite. You don't have to ask how my wife or the kids are doing, just ask politely. "Hi. How are you? Good. Listen I'm calling to find out if there's anything available in the room." When I call up a club myself, I say, "Hi. How are you doing? Good. I have a note on my calendar reminding me that you wanted me to call to see if we could possibly find some open dates together during the next couple of months." Have a pleasant tone. Get good phone manners. It's very important.

Also, learn who you are talking to and be polite to them. You may not actually be talking to the booking agent. You may be talking to an assistant. Well you better be nice to them and polite to them because if you're not, they're the gatekeeper. They'll never get you to the booking agent, so be polite.

If you're dealing with the staff when you get to the club, be polite. I see so many comics say, "She's just the waitress," or "He's only the bartender. I just need to be polite to the manager or the owner." Wrong. If you're not polite to the serving staff believe me, it will come back to haunt you. And if you're asking "Why? What can they do to me?" Well, what you don't realize is that maybe one of the waitresses is dating the booker, or is married to the owner. You don't know the dynamics of what's going on in that club. More importantly, if you piss off the staff in general, they will get back at you. I've seen it happen.

The serving staff are usually just young kids probably around 18 to 24, and they're there trying to make money. If you're a jerk to them, here's what can happen. Their job, if they do it well, is to get drinks and food to the audience. If they do it well while you're onstage, what they do is say as softly as possible, "Excuse me, would anyone at this table like any more drinks, or are you all set? Okay, great, thanks! I'll be back in a little bit." That's doing you a favor, and also doing a good job. Why? Because they're not disturbing the room, they're trying to get orders from just that one table. Only that table is being slightly disturbed at that point.

If they don't like you and they don't care, they'll literally just stand up. They won't crouch down, and they'll just talk loud, like, "You guys want any more drinks here? Do you want a Heineken? Do you want me to refill that? Do you want any water?" Well, all of a sudden, they're standing up, which is interfering with my show, because now people are looking at the server and not at me. They're also not only interfering with that table, but the table next to them, the table behind them, the table in front of them, the tables to the sides of them. They're disturbing about 25-30 people instead of just four.

They can get back at you. So why not just be polite? Always remember to say "Please" and "Thank You." It is amazing to me, not only just in comedy, but in general, people have forgotten "pleases" and "thank you." It's so much easier to work with pleasant people than it is to work with jerks. Believe me, I have hired people that are slightly less funny, just because they're easier to work with. Those people will always work more than the people who are jerks. Unless you're the funniest person in the world and we just can't have a show without you, you'd better learn "please" and "thank you."

15

Call to Confirm

Another important attribute of being a professional is always calling to confirm that you're going to be at the show. If it's an in-town show and the club is five minutes away, maybe you can just drop by. It's not a big deal. But because most clubs aren't within five minutes, so it should be very easy to pick up a phone and say something like, "Hi, this is Barry Neal. I just want to make sure you know that I'm going to be there at 8:30 for my 9 o'clock spot. Oh good, we're all set? See you then! Thank you!"

Another reason you should call to confirm is to avoid a common problem: sometimes bookers inadvertently book two people for the same spot. It's called double booking. It stinks, but it happens – and if it does, when you get to the club you discover that they've hired somebody else, or they don't even have your name at all on the books. Make the call. It only costs pennies, and can save you a lot of time.

You also definitely want to call when it's an out-of-town gig. If you have to fly to Wisconsin to do a show in Milwaukee and you're living in L.A. - well, why don't you call the club a few days before and just say something like, "Hi, this is Barry Neal. Just calling to confirm I'm coming to Milwaukee, and would like to know where you want me to go when I get to the airport?" That tells them that you're definitely going to be there – something they probably had no doubts about, but appreciate your extra effort in putting them at ease.

In addition to letting them know that you really know how to take care of business, when I get there, you won't be struggling to find out where the hotel is, or where the condominium is, or where the club is. You get all those answers right then and there, during the call. I would usually also say, "Oh great, you want me to take a cab to the hotel and you'll reimburse me at the show? Great!" Now, they're at ease knowing we're all on the same page. I know how to get to the hotel. We're all set.

And if you don't do that, here's what might happen. You show up -- and this happened to me. This is why I'm telling you to call. I flew out to Buffalo, New York. That's where my in-laws are. Thank goodness I like my in-laws. I stayed at their house. They picked me up at the airport, and I drove to the show, which was in a hotel, and I go to where the club was. I'd already showcased there. The room was dark, and looked like it was locked. I went up to the hotel manager and was told, "Yeah, we haven't done comedy for two weeks. The guy took off with all our money." I said, "Nobody called me." He said, "We thought he would. What do we care?" And I was stuck. I was stuck in Buffalo. Thank goodness my in-laws were there, or I would have just flown up to Buffalo for no reason.

Things like that can *and do* happen. Believe me, it happens more times than you want to know. Thank goodness I learned from that and started calling. Another time I called up -- it was in Syracuse, New York. Sure enough, I called up a week before, and said, "Hi, this is Barry Neal. I'm going to be your headliner this week." And they said, "We don't even have you on the books." I said, "Excuse me?" They said, "Yeah, we don't have you on the books." And I said, "I was booked six months ago." And they said, "Oh yeah, you were with the old booking agent. We fired him." I said, "You fired him? But you didn't tell me!" And they said "Well, we just assumed he would call all those people." And I'm thinking, "Why would he call? You fired him. He doesn't care what happens to us." So, I could have flown to Syracuse to find out I'm not even booked. Again, it's a cheap phone call. Just pennies, if you have a good plan. Call ahead.

And the final reason you want to call ahead is that it puts them at ease knowing you've flown in. Once I arrive in town, I call the club and say, "Hi, this is Barry Neal. I'm at the hotel. Showtime's at 8 o'clock, and I'll see you by 7:30. Thank you." Bang. It's that easy.

Here's another story of why someone got fired because they just didn't think and act like a professional. I'm in Provo, Utah at a club. A good friend of mine owns the club and I'm there with my wife. We're vacationing. We're going skiing, and I just wanted to stop in and say hello. And it's about 7:30 and he says to me, he says, "Barry, I haven't heard from the headline. Can you stay and headline the show if I don't hear from him?" I said, "Sure, I'll do whatever you want, Johnny." And, I stayed until 7:45 and he said, "You know what? I don't know where he is." And he's having a nervous attack because his headliner's not there, 15 minutes before show. He doesn't even know if he's in town.

Finally, at 8:00 o'clock, he starts the show. The headliner's not supposed to go on until about 8:40, but it's already 8 o'clock. The show is starting, and the headliner's not there. At 8:15 I am ready to go on. I'm preparing my set. The headliner strolls in, so nonchalant, and goes "Hey, so when am I going on, in like 20 minutes?" The owner says, "Where were you?" He said, "Oh, I was just at the hotel getting ready." He ended up doing the show, got a lot of laughs, was a good headliner, and my friend who owns the club just told me, "I am never bringing this guy back. I almost had a heart attack!"

Always call ahead. It's the courteous thing to do. And remember to be polite. Try to step into someone else's shoes. If you're the club owner, you want to know your performer is definitely going to be there, so just use common sense. It goes a long way.

16

No Surprises

Another sign of a real professional is not surprising bookers. Surprise parties are great, but people in the professional world do not like surprises. They want things to run just as expected. If I'm a booker who sees you at a show and I say "Hey, I think you're funny, could you come do my show?" When I'm booking you off of what I see, whether it's a tape or I see you in person, that's what I expect. So when you come and do my show, I want to see that same set. Of course you might change a joke here or there a little bit, but I don't want to see a whole different persona. I don't want you to go, "Oh, by the way, you know that set I did, I now do a Kabuki play." I'm not hiring a Kabuki play. My headliner's not a Kabuki act. I don't want chimes and makeup. I want the funny set I saw you do, that's what I hired. Don't surprise me. Do what got you booked.

This is especially important when it comes to TV shows. You must be prepared. Don't surprise executives. Nothing angers them more than when you're not prepared. When we shot the MTV show, I went to New York a few days ahead of time and did my set over and over and over, the same set over and over. Well, we got to the rehearsal a few hours before the show and the casting person said, "Oh, is everyone ready with their set?" and there were a couple of people who said, "I haven't decided what I'm going to do yet." I'm thinking, "Wow, that is really gutsy. You haven't thought about what you're going to do? Showtime's in like three hours!" Sure enough, one of the people who wasn't prepared started doing his set, and as I'm standing next to the person who booked the show, she's having a heart attack. I'm thinking, "He's doing okay." And she tells me, "He's doing some of the same material that he did from another set from MTV." This was MTV's half-hour comedy hour.

The reason his MTV performance bothered the booker is because the rule of thumb is: when you do material on a network, you don't repeat that material on the same network. So when I would do *Evening at the Improvs*, you would always look at the prior *Evening at the Improvs* to make sure you're not duplicating the material. They had to throw out everything he said that was duplicated, so out of his six-minute set, they could only use two minutes. He never worked for them again, of course. So once more: don't surprise people. Be prepared and let them know that you're ready. Surprise parties? Good. Surprising people onstage? Not good.

17

<u>R-E-S-P-E-C-T</u>

Being a professional also means treating everyone with respect, and expecting to be treated with respect in return. Now first, why should you treat people with respect? Well, hello? It's the right thing to do. But two, you just don't know who you're disrespecting. The amount of times a bartender or a waitress becomes a booking agent is alarming. There's no school you have to attend to be a booker. I'm a booker. I was (and still am) a comic. Believe me, I will never use any comic who's ever pissed me off. Maybe I hold grudges, but there are too many good people out there who would like to work for you... you don't have to use some jerk. Be respectful to the bartender. Be respectful to the serving staff. Not only can they endanger your show, but one of them just might become the booking agent. Bottom line: be respectful. It's real easy.

And in return, you should also be treated with respect. So many times young comics, because of their age, feel as though they don't deserve the same respect

131

everyone else gets. Nonsense, we're all people, okay? If I'm headlining and I want a glass of water, I get up and get a glass of water, okay? I don't look at my opening act and go, "Hey listen, go get me some water, Thanks." Now, if you're getting up, I'll say, "Hey, could you get me a glass of water while you're up?" But of course, I'd do the same. If I'm getting up, I'll look around and say, "Hey, can I get you a glass of water?" So be treated with respect.

There are rungs of the ladder of stand-up that you do have to abide by. One is if you're in a condominium and you're sharing it, the headliner does get the top room. I'll cover the condominium rules in the next chapter. So there are certain things that you have to abide by, but in general, be treated with respect. Too many times people will talk down to you. You're human. You don't have to put up with that.

There's a certain booking agent who books a lot of rooms in Vegas, and his M.O. is to be vulgar and humiliate you. I talked to him a few times and finally said, "You know what? I'm very happy with who I am. I don't need to be spoken to like that," and I hung up the phone. And I've never worked for him. And fine. I don't want to work for jerks. You have to decide where your barometer is, and you can't have a real low threshold because it's a tough business. But you also don't have to be humiliated, okay? So stand up straight and treat people with respect. I think when you stand up and you stand your ground, I think people will respect you for that.

One of the things that I do when I treat people with respect is I give them stuff, because the staff, they are the core that makes the show work. So at the end of the week, I used to offer to take the staff out to dinner. Because the show went so late, most of them never took me up on it. So I would give them a nice tip. Everyone gets a tip, the bartender, all the waitresses, if they've worked a few days, I give them tips. Now you're saying, "Wait a minute. That's not respect. That's a bribe!" You're right! It's a bribe, and that's okay. It's worth it for me, for me as the headliner, to pay out $40 or $50 in tips so at the end of the week or on Monday when they have their team meeting and they say, "Hey, what did you guys think of Barry Neal?" I guarantee you everyone who got a nice tip says "I thought he was great! We can't wait to have Barry Neal back!" It's real simple. It doesn't cost a whole lot, and it's worth it because I know every year I'm welcomed back at that club. So I'm not saying you have to tip people more than you can afford, but at least if you're respectful and you're nice and you get along with them, at least you have good rapport and that's good, because at the end of the week, they have their meeting and you want them to say, "We liked him! We want him back!"

18

Condo Rules

When you get booked in a room on the road away from home, you will stay in one of two places: either a hotel, or the club's condominium. If given the choice, a hotel is preferable because you get to stay in the room by yourself, turn the TV to a favorite program, turn the air conditioning on, and do whatever you want. It's your room and you don't have to share it with anyone else. Most comics prefer that.

In the alternative, the club may put you up in a condominium or an apartment. That can be nice, because the apartment no doubt has a kitchenette with a stove, so some people prefer that because they like to cook their food and have meals in. I don't. I like the hotel. However, when I can't stay in one and I have to stay in an apartment, you cannot bring guests, okay? If you have a girlfriend and you want her to stay, she simply can't stay in the condo. It's not fair.

If there are three people staying in there, it's not fair that you bring someone else. It's already crowded enough if there are two people in the apartment or three people, because you don't know the other two people. It's not fair that someone brings their girlfriend. Now I have to listen to you guys fighting, you guys having sex. I don't want any of it, okay? It's hard enough to get along with two other people. Don't bring in a third party that doesn't need to be there, especially because sometimes there will be hard feelings.

I was in a room one time and I'm headlining, and this guy brought his girlfriend, and he left during Sunday. He went out jogging or something, and she's stuck in the condo, and I don't know this person. You know, and this is where I have to be. I am living here for the week, or at least four or five days. And I told her, Sunday at 12 o'clock the Bears game goes on. And she said, "Well hold on. I'm watching this movie." I said, "That's really not my concern. You don't have to be here. You should be out with your boyfriend. I'm sorry, but this is my home, and there's only one TV." And the Bears game went on at 12:00. She probably thought I was a jerk, and maybe you think, "Aw, that's kind of rude," but you know what? You can't bring a guest into the condo. Those are the rules.

Don't bring your girlfriend unless it's a pre-arranged agreement between you and the other comic, that you each know and you each bring your girlfriend, or whatever.

And also, don't bring guests back from the club. If you meet someone at the club and you're single and you want to go, "Hey, let's all go back to the condo and party," it's not fair to the other comic. Look, I just want to sit quietly. I want to get on my computer. I want to watch Sports Center. I don't want you guys partying in the condo.

So just try to get along in an amicable way. If you smoke, be cognizant if the other person doesn't. Go out onto the patio and smoke, or just smoke in your particular room. Don't smoke in the general area. Again, be polite, be conscientious, and don't trash the condo. If the condo gets trashed, you're both responsible, and you both won't work for that club again.

19

Doing Your Time

Being a professional means doing your time onstage. Don't ever go over your time. I'm going to say this again, really slow: *Never go over your time.* A lot of comics think, "Oh well, I'm doing great. I know I was told to do five, but the audience loves me. I'm doing ten!" Wrong. You've done 100% more time than I asked for. I may not ever use you again. Don't do it. A show has to flow a certain way. The reason I gave you ten minutes, or five minutes is because the show has to end in ninety minutes. So if the opener's supposed to do fifteen, and the feature's supposed to do thirty, and the headliner's doing forty-five, that's what I want.

If the opener does twenty, that's not good because now the feature does his thirty, and the headliner only gets forty. Or let's say the opener does twenty instead of fifteen, and the feature does thirty-five instead of thirty. Well now instead of doing forty-five, he's doing thirty-five. He's barely headlining the room. He's doing only five minutes more than the feature, and that's not what I want. The headliner gets the most money because he's probably the best act on the bill. He's the person the people come out to see, so don't ever go over your time.

How do you know when you go over your time? Wear a watch, if you want. In every room, there's a red light in the back that tells you when to get off stage. We're going to talk about that a little bit later in another section of the book. But you have to know how much time you are doing.

The rule of thumb is basically this: you have a ten percent window of opportunity to get on or off. What do I mean by that? If I say do ten minutes, given ten percent leeway, ten percent of ten is one. So you have a nine minute to eleven minute window. See how that works? Ten percent of ten is one. If you do nine, you can do eleven. No one is going to say anything. You start doing twelve, that's a little bit more time than I wanted. You do fifteen - well, I said do ten, not fifteen. You're doing fifty percent more than I wanted you to do. That's huge! Think about it: if you got a fifty percent raise at work, you'd be thrilled! That's way too much. Nobody gets a fifty percent raise, except for ball players.

And don't use the excuse, "But I was killing!" Well, of course you were! That's why I hired you. That's why anyone hires you. Of course you're doing well. We expect you to do well. If you don't do well, then we have a real problem. If you go over your time and you're not doing well, you're fired. So don't come offstage saying, "Hey, the audience loved me." Too bad. I don't care. It has to be set for a certain amount of time for each person. Don't go over your time. Trust me, you'll get fired faster than anything else by being unprofessional and doing too much time.

20

The Press Package

Once you're a professional, you must put together a media including résumés, head shots, and a tape or DVD. These are the three things that you must have in your press package.

Let's start with the résumé. You should have one that looks good, and it has to be on computer paper. I can't believe how many comics who think, "I'll just write out my stuff." Writing it out? Think about going to IBM or Hewlett-Packard. Are you going to send them a résumé in crayon? You might as well do that. "I am very funny. Please hire me. Here is my..." No! Get a computer. We're in the new millennium, my friends. Get a computer. Put your résumé on computer-printed paper.

You may ask, "What do I put on my résumé. I haven't worked any clubs!" Lie! Lie! Just make sure they're good lies. No one's going to hire you if you have on your résumé, "Well, I've never actually worked at a club, but I'd like to work yours!" Don't put

141

down coffee houses. Put down clubs that maybe you've done guest sets in. Put down clubs that you've frequented as a patron. I'm not saying lying is good, but you have to be able to put little white lies in so that people are comfortable hiring you.

A résumé may not *get* you a job, but it can *prevent* you from getting one. Quite frankly, if I look at a résumé and don't see any comedy clubs, why would I put him in my comedy club? I'm thinking you've never done a comedy club. So again, comics can help you. Teachers can help you put little white lies in. Just to make the booker feel pretty confident. They're not going to check. They don't care.

So many comics ask, "What if they check?" Do you think I have time to check on everyone's résumé? If you're coming to me wanting to be an opening act or a feature act, and you say you've headlined in Butte, Montana, or you headlined in St. Louis, do you think I'm going to call St. Louis? "Hi, do you know Phil Johnson? Did he ever work for you?" It never happens - ever. So put down comedy clubs that you think they're not going to check. Just don't put down a comedy club that you're trying to get into. And certainly don't attempt a ridiculous lie. Don't put down, "I headlined Caesar's Palace!" Really? And you're trying to get in to be an opener here in Kokomo? Hmm, that's kind of odd. Make them little white lies, but just lies that feel comfortable, so if asked you can say, "Yeah, I've worked those clubs." Just hope they don't ask if you were onstage or the janitor.

Okay, now that we have our résumé set, you need a head shot. A head shot is an 8" X 10" photo that is basically a picture of you. But you need a head shot that says something about you. Don't just get a regular head shot, "That's me!" I try to have my head shots say something. I'm in a suit and tie. I have "Barry Neal, Counselor of Love," so when people see my head shot, they go, "Oh, we're probably going to see something professional, maybe intelligent, based on relationships." Your head shot should say, just like what you're wearing onstage, your head shot should say something about you. I had a guy, a comic, gave me a head shot with a toilet plunger on his head. Well, I pretty much extrapolated what I'm going to get. You're going to get a guy who does props, with toilet plungers on his head, and kind of silly and juvenile, and that's exactly what I got. So when you think about doing a head shot, think about it in terms of what you're wearing, and what your pose is, and it should say a little bit about your act. That's your head shot.

We're set with our résumé. We're set with our head shot. Now you need a demo tape or DVD. This is something you're going to need to show somebody. This is what I do. Now a tape or DVD will almost never get you a job, because quite frankly, people don't look at tapes and go, "Wow, you're funny" because again, you're rarely ever funny on tape. You really need to see the person. But, although tapes may not get you the job, much like a bad résumé, it can possible *prevent* you from getting a job.

If someone says, "Hire this guy," I'll go, "I'll give him a chance," and then I see the tape and it's terrible, I won't work them. If it's a passable tape I'll work them, especially with a good referral.

So, what's a good demo? A good demo is you, on a stage, with good lights, good microphone, and a good audience. Don't send a tape from a coffee house. What your tape says is, "This is the best work I've ever done. This represents my best." If I see that and say, "Your best is a coffee house? And you're calling me to work my club? My club that seats 300 people, which is a dinner theatre, with headliners from The Tonight Show, Letterman and their own TV shows. And you want to work it because you've done a coffee house?" No chance. Nobody is going to hire you if your best work is at a coffee house, so if that's all you've got, don't send it.

Visit a comedy club. There's got to be some local club that's near you, within an hour or two, and say "I can get five or ten people." Bring your audience, bring your friends, bring your family. "Give me five to ten minutes." Tape that show. And now you have a tape from a legitimate show. It's The Ice House, The Improv, whatever, The Funny Bone. As long as there's some club identification on the wall behind you, it says that, people will go, "At least he's been at a club."

Have a demo that is recent. I saw a tape of a guy who said, "Oh, you know, just ignore the material, I don't do that stuff anymore." I'm not a mind reader like Kreskin. I can't just imagine you doing different material. I can only see what I see. So if the tape is not recent, don't send it out. And again, make sure it looks good with the lighting. Believe it or not, this guy sent me a tape and wanted to get work. I looked at the tape and I said, "Was this done in your basement? It looks terrible!" And he said, "Well, it was my garage." And I was kidding with him! I'm like, "Well, who's laughing?" He said, "That's my family." I said, "You can't send this tape out. No one is going to hire you because your best work is in your garage. You know, why don't you just set up a camera at work and tell jokes to your co-workers?"

Send out a demo that's from a club. Send out a demo that is recent. Send out a demo that shows your best material with a good response from a good audience...One that represents your best work.

Summing up, have a good résumé. If you have to put in a few white lies, go ahead. Have a head shot that says something about you. Have a decent demo tape or DVD from a decent club, and you're on your way to working professionally.

21

<u>Work On Your Weaknesses</u>

Now that you're a professional, you have to be your own toughest critic. In order to improve, you cannot trust unconditional supporters. Your friends and your family are great. They love you and they want you to be the best, but just by saying, "Hey, my friends think I'm great" is not good enough. You have to know what your weaknesses are and work on them. The great ones always do. Great comics become great because they risk. They risk failing, and then when they fail, they get better.

Again, I go back to Michael Jordan, who's my favorite. He won six championships. He worked on his weaknesses. Michael, coming out of the University of North Carolina, had a bad outside shot. So what did he do? He didn't just work on his dunking, of course, that's easy. What was hard was working on that outside shot, again and again, and doing that fade-away that he did that nobody could ever stop. So when he was ready, and he had Scottie

Pippen and Horace Grant, they won their championships, he was unstoppable. He had no weaknesses.

That's what you have to do. Know your weaknesses and work on them. It's the only way you're going to become better. Because what happens is if you think, "I don't work well with the audience," start working with the audience. Slowly, get better. And all of a sudden, your working with the audience stops being a weakness and becomes a strength.

"I don't do physical stuff very well." Work on it. "I don't handle the microphone well." Work on it. So, in the ledger, all these weaknesses become strengths. And pretty soon, all your strengths are there and you have no weaknesses, and you feel confident because you can walk into any room, anywhere, any time, and you know there's nothing that can throw you. You have too many strengths.

22

<u>Write-Offs</u>

If you're going to be a professional, start writing off some of the stuff that you're paying for. This may just be a little side business now, but you purchased this book. Write it off. Check with your local accountant. I believe you have two years to start up a business. So, take all the stuff that you've put into this business, even though it's a side business, because you want this to be your business. So the book that you buy – tax write-off. The classes that you take – tax write-off. The mileage that you drive to a club, those coffee houses, to the open mics, the mileage is a tax write-off. Think about those things. Don't just say, "Oh, it's okay. It doesn't matter." This is your *business*. You're a professional. Start writing stuff off.

Last thing I want to mention is <u>never pay to perform</u>. Sometimes coffee houses will say, "Hey, if you can buy a donut, it keeps us around in business because otherwise we wouldn't be open this day."

At least if it's up front, you may say, "Well, okay," because it's on a Monday night, and normally they're not open. They're not making any money because no one's there except for the comics, so every comic buys a donut or a cup of coffee. That's not a big deal.

But don't pay to perform and say, "Sure, I'll pay you $10 if you let me on your stage," or "Hey, it's a contest. I only have to pay $25 to enter." Those are nothing but scams. You are the artist. You should be getting paid to perform. In the beginning, no one's going to pay you, and that's okay, because you're working on your craft. But if someone tells you, "Hey, I have a cable access show and you just have to pay $50 and I'll tape you and you'll be on a talk show on cable access," that's nonsense. They get it for free. It's a scam. They do that to enough people, and they make money. Be very careful. Not everyone is forthright and honest. That may come as a shock. Hopefully it doesn't. Don't pay to perform. Go up there, learn your craft, work for free, get better, and eventually you're the one who's going to get paid.

That's pretty much what we have to say bout professionalism. We've covered a lot of ground. Hopefully now you can understand how to start finding your voice. And hopefully, you've learned a little bit. Hopefully you already knew it, about how to be a professional. When you get those two things, you've found your voice and you act like a professional, you're going to start getting work and you're going to start getting paid.

In the next Section we're going to discuss "Analyzing the Audience." The more you know about the audience, the better off you are, the stronger you'll become. And we're going to give you some tips on how to analyze the audience, how to break down where they are, how to deal with them. Because without the audience, you don't have a show. They're the third element of stand-up: Material, Delivery, and Audience.

Comedy Career Management by Barry Neal

SECTION III:
ANALYZING THE AUDIENCE

1

Introduction

Here in Section Three we're going to discuss how to analyze the audience. The audience, again, is one of the three basic required elements of your stand-up comedy routine, the first being material, the second being delivery, and the third being the audience.

We want to analyze the audience because the more you know about them the better off you'll be. So for the next hour or so we're going to sit back and we're going to tell you some tips on how to analyze the audience so you know more about them so you can work an interact better for them.

2

Grab Attention & Pull Focus

Let's say that the emcee just introduced you. The audience is ready for you. Now what? First, the most important thing you have to do is grab the audience's attention and pull the focus of the room towards you. Again, we'll go back to that utopian world where you're introduced, "It's Barry Neal," and the audience politely applauds and then sits quietly just waiting for your brilliance to come across.

That's not the way it in works the real world. More often than not, you'll be introduced and get a small smattering of applause, or maybe they won't applaud at all, or they'll be doing something else. They might still be whispering about how great (or lousy) that other comic who opened for you was.

Well, what are you going to do? Your job is to make sure that you have complete focus on you. You cannot get started until the audience is ready to start. Otherwise if you just start talking and the audience isn't paying attention, you become a substitute teacher. Remember substitute teachers? Nobody paid attention to them. They're on the blackboard. They're doing things. They never commanded respect. You have to command that respect.

So, what do you do? There is no one way to do it. You have to find your own voice. As you're introduced you might want to grab the microphone and go, "Alright folks. Sit back and relax. I'm captaining this ship. My name is Barry Neal. If any of you get out of line, you're going overboard. Thank you very much." If they don't applaud, just go, "Thank you very much for not applauding. Now this time, I want you to applaud," and demand they applaud. You tell them what to do and they'll do it.

One of the best opening moves I ever saw was by a guy named Stanley Olman. He would be introduced at the Improv and it's very difficult to go up at the Improv unless you're a very big name, because the audience, their expectations, they always want to see the big act. They want to see Jerry Seinfeld walk in. They want to see Jay Leno walk in. So when you're not a name they recognize, they're like 'ugh'.

So what he would do, he'd be introduced and there'd be a little applause but people would still be talking at their table, ordering drinks, talking about the last act they just saw. He'd walk up on stage and just stand in front of the microphone. Ten, 15 seconds. He'd have a cup of coffee. He'd take a sip, place the coffee down. After 15 seconds, people who were kind of chatting and talking were looking going, "What is this guy doing?" After 30 seconds of not saying anything, all of a sudden all of the heads were turning going, "When is this guy going to say something?" He'd take his glasses off, clean them off, check them out.

He was on stage 45 seconds to a minute without even addressing the audience. Well you can just imagine after 30 seconds the audience was captivated by this. After 45 seconds they were on the edge of their seats going, "What is going on?" Finally, after he felt it was time, he'd hit them with the punch line. "What are you looking at? When you go to work, do you start right away?" Boom! The audience was laughing and he had them in complete control. From that point on, he let them know 'I'm in control. The pace of the show will be at my pace, not yours.' It's a lot like training a dog.

- -

[editor's note]

An old-time comedian named Irwin Corey would come out onstage with a three-day beard, and dressed in a ragged tuxedo. For the first full minute he would silently look around at the audience, as if he was deep in thought.

Finally, after the silence had become deafening, he would look down at the crowd and forcefully utter his first words: "And furthermore..." The audience went crazy with laughter.

- - - - - - - - - - - - - - - - - - - -

Grab their attention. Grab it from this end. Grab it from that end and pull the focus towards you so everyone is watching you. Once you have their attention, if your material and your delivery is decent, you'll be fine.

3

How're Ya Doin'?

One of the worst things you can do just after you've been introduced is grab the microphone and open with, "Hey! How's everyone doing out there?" That's a big mistake. Too many bad comics start their act out with a 'How are you doing.' Here's what the problem with that is. What you're doing is asking a question to an audience that isn't sure what's going on. They don't have faith that you're funny, so what do you want from them? You're asking a question. In a perfect world, when you ask how you're doing, they'd say, "Yay! We're doing fine. Now let's be funny."

The problem is, it doesn't happen like that. By asking a question, you're giving away control. The only control you have is that microphone. I can speak when I want to. If I ask the question, "Hey, how are you doing", what I'm really doing is saying, 'you now have the control. You tell me where we're going.' The audience can't lead the ship. You have to lead the ship. You must have that authority.

You cannot let someone question your authority, so don't give up that control. The control you have is in the microphone, and the power that you can speak when you want to, and they really have to listen. You need to steer the ship.

By asking questions, you're losing control. Don't start out by losing control. It creates anarchy. Come on out and start with your bit. Do what you need to do to establish that you are in control and you're going to be funny.

4

The Joke Bombed

Okay, now you're on stage and you have control of the room. You do a bit and the bit bombs. What next? The point here is, who cares? The audience doesn't have your script. Maybe that particular joke was a set up. Maybe it wasn't supposed to be funny. Don't act as if the joke bombed and you feel bad about it.

There are several reasons why we don't admit the joke bombed. First, if we admit the joke bombed, then what we're saying is that we are doing jokes and we're trying to manipulate you into laughing. Instead you should get them to believe that you're trying to have a dialogue... a conversation. "I just thought of this. Maybe it's not funny, but I just thought of that. Isn't that interesting?"

So by saying the joke bombed, what you're really telling them is, "I'm doing a series of set bits that hopefully you will laugh at." It takes the audience out of the rhythm and relaxation of, "Ah, we're just talking." Now all of a sudden they're sitting up waiting, going "What's the next joke? Is that joke going to be funny?"

The other problem with saying a joke bombed is now you're saying, "I prepared something. It wasn't funny. I apologize." You'll sometimes see people go, "Well, I'm not going to do that bit again." Don't. Don't apologize for a joke. The joke didn't go well. Who cares? "I did the joke because I thought the joke was funny. I still think the joke is funny and I think you, as the audience, missed out." That's what I'm thinking. Granted in the back of my head, I'm noting, "Okay. That joke didn't get a laugh." If it happens enough times, I stop doing the joke. But if a joke bombs, nobody knows.

A lot of times, you may think the joke bombed and it didn't. Maybe something happened. Maybe a drink dropped. Maybe someone was ordering food too loud. Maybe a cell phone went off. There are a lot of things that could happen. So don't sit there and admit that a joke bombed because, you're admitting one, that you failed. You never want to give that up. You never want to say, "I failed at something" because now the audience will question your authority.

And two, you don't want to admit that you're just doing jokes because the audience will sit back and judge you; and you don't want the audience to do that.

5

No Apologies

I've mentioned a joke not going well. If it bombs, what do you do? If you apologize for a joke, you are making a grave mistake, because the captain of a ship never apologizes for the orders he gives. Again, privately, he may go into his quarters and think, "That was a mistake." But at the time, the crew needs to have confidence that the captain knows what he's doing. As the stand-up, you're captain of the ship. You're leading the way. The audience is your crew. You never apologize unless you hurt somebody's feelings, and then you might say, "Hey, I'm sorry. I stepped out of line." But if you're doing a joke, you can't apologize.

I always think of Captain Kirk on *Star Trek*. If he says photon torpedoes, you don't see Sulu turn around and go, "Are you sure want photon torpedoes, because in my opinion..." Hey, I'm the captain. What I say goes. Don't ever question my authority. I know what I'm doing. It inspires confidence in the crew and that's what happens in the audience.

The audience needs to know that you're in control... that you know what you're doing, so they can relax. And when they relax, they stop thinking. You don't want an audience thinking too much about every joke, because if you overanalyze jokes they're not funny. Relax. Have a good time. Don't question my authority. And your authority will not be questioned if you don't apologize.

Never sit there and say, "Well, that was a new joke. Sorry about that." What happens when you do that is now the audience then sits up. Their antennas go up and thinking "Wow, he apologized once, so maybe we can sway him to apologize again." The audience now becomes the judge, jury and executioner on every one of your bits.

Unacceptable. The audience is there, and in my opinion for three things: you can laugh; you can applaud; or you can not laugh. You cannot judge my jokes. Have a good time. If you admit you're failing, you're admitting you're doing jokes. Believe me, the audience will sit up and just say, "Nah, okay, that was a good joke." Then they'll sit back again and go, "I think that one needs some work." It makes a real bad recipe for a show. You don't ever want the audience judging. You want them relaxed, confident, saying, "You're running the ship. You lead the way. We'll sit back. We'll just have a good time." So again, be the captain. Don't ever apologize for what you've done on stage, because if you didn't mean to do it, then you shouldn't have done it in the first place. But if you meant to say it because you thought it was funny, stand by it. Stand by your jokes.

There are some people who can get away with apologizing for a joke. If you've established yourself in that first 30 minutes on stage and the audience is confident that you're funny and you lay an egg, you do a new joke that totally bombs, you just go, "Wow. That was a new bit. Let's not do that again" and it might get a laugh. And the audience will give you a mulligan. It's a golf term. It's a do-over. "It's okay. We know you're funny. You did a bad one. Just don't let it keep happening." That can work, because you've already inspired confidence.

That's why when you see monologues by established superstars, Johnny Carson was the master of it, Jay Leno, Letterman, these are stars very experienced in doing monologue, so when a joke doesn't go well, they'll look to their head writer and go, "Hey, you owe me the $50 on that", and it's funny, because we know these people are funny. They have their own TV show. They don't have to apologize in sincerity because we know they're funny. They get the benefit of the doubt. But if you're just starting out and you're not sure if you have that confidence, don't apologize. You're making a bad decision.

6

Handling Hecklers

Unfortunately, when you start doing shows and dealing with audiences, you're going to run across some hecklers. Hecklers are people that try to interfere with the show. They talk too loud. They say things back to you, and you have to deal with them. And you have to deal with them swiftly and mostly sternly. What a heckler is being, more often than not, is what I call a mutineer. They're creating a mutiny in the audience. They're trying to get the audience to get together and go, "We don't think you're funny" or "I'm funnier than this comic. That's why I'm saying things."

Well, guess what, Fletcher Christian? I'm Captain Bligh, and I'm putting a stop to it. You cannot let a mutiny occur. So if somebody's heckling, you better put them down and put them down fast...and the only way to put them down fast and make sure that they stay down is to establish your credibility. There are hundreds of things that you can say to hecklers that put them down. You can get them in almost any comedy book, but a lot of them are like "Hey, I don't go where you work and tell you how to run the frying machine." "Hey when your IQ reaches 80, sell." "This is what happens when a fetus doesn't get enough oxygen." It's a lot of stock lines. "Hey when you went to school, did you ride the big bus or the little bus?" My personal favorite, "Hey, shouldn't you be at home writing letters to Jodie Foster?" There are hundreds of them, and you'll hear them all the time.

But these insults will only work if you have established credibility as the funniest person in the room. This is why I'm going to emphasize, when you start your show, start out strong. Start out with a killer first few minutes because what will happen is that the audience will relax and go, "Oh, this person's funny." And if somebody heckles and says, "I don't think he's funny", the rest of the audience will be on your side, because you've established yourself as funny.

So now you have that credibility. I'm funny. The people want to listen to me. Somebody stands up or somebody yells something at you, you can easily put them down with any stock line and the audience will laugh and applaud and make fun of that person for trying to interfere with your show. You have to get the audience on your side. Establish credibility. That's the key to dealing with hecklers.

There are two types of hecklers. The first type is what I call the ignorant heckle. They don't know they're heckling. They're just having a good time. Sometimes they're repeating your joke or if I do a joke about my wife and the car keys, losing her car keys, they'll just kind of point to their wife and kind of go, "My wife does the same." I don't consider that a belligerent heckle. They're just having a good time. They're trying to show me that they're involved and that they agree with what I'm saying. They still need to be put down, but I put them down gently, because they're not trying to be malicious. They're not trying to harm the show. So normally I'll just say to them, "You know what? If I need your help, I'll call on you," or something like, "You know, I've done my show thousands of times. It really works well when you don't say anything." It's basically a nice, polite way of saying, "Shut the hell up. I'm doing okay." More often than not, they get it. They're just so enthusiastic, you don't want to lay into them really hard.

And then sometimes you'll get what's called a belligerent heckler. They're most probably drunk and tired. They're jealous that you're on stage making the girlfriend laugh. What they want to do is upset you. They want to tell you 'you suck', 'you're not funny'. They just want to talk loud at their table to show that they're a macho man, whatever it is. These people have to be put down swiftly and harshly. Again, if you've established credibility, you can use the rest of the audience against them.

Oftentimes, a couple of these good hard put-downs can shut them up. If not, you can get the audience together and just go, "Hey, how about on the count of 3, we tell this guy to shut the hell up? One, Two, Three." And the whole audience, if they're on your side, will say, "Shut the hell up". Then you can look at him and just go, "Now, who's in control?"

Both types of hecklers have to be put down. Belligerent hecklers are the worst. Sometimes you need to kick them out. We'll get into that a little bit later. Other than that, there are times where it's okay to leave the show.

Comedy Career Management by **Barry Neal**

Sometimes it's very funny when you don't care. One of the best lines I ever heard was David Spade. We were working in Vegas together and there were these two guys who really were drunk and just obnoxious businessmen, and they were talking through David's set. Finally David looked at them and said, "What's the problem?" And one of the guys says, "We don't think you're funny." And David just said, "Good, because if you thought I was funny I'd quit the business right f'ing now." And that showed the rest of the audience, 'I don't care. I don't care if you don't think I'm funny. I think I'm funny.' So that's a great way to handle a situation. Don't try to suck up to the heckler. Don't try to apologize for not being funny. Get in their face and tell them, "Hey, I'm in control. Shut up. I have credibility."

Once you've established credibility and put the heckler down, what now? Well, it's important that you stop talking to the heckler. So many times, if you put a heckler down, you'll do your show and you just can't help yourself. You want to get another jab in. Don't. You've put him down. They've shut up. Don't keep going back to them. If you have a joke about someone acting like an idiot, "You know, I was at the bank and this person was an idiot." Well that guy knows what I'm talking about. Don't do it. The audience has already seen you put them down. Don't drag them back into the show because quite frankly, if you start talking to them again, you deserve to be heckled again. Stop talking to them.

There are times when you have to be honest, because if you haven't established credibility with the audience and someone has heckled you, what are you going to do? That can happen. I was in El Paso, Texas and I was on after a very tough act to follow - a high-energy black guy who did Michael Jackson impressions. He was really very funny, and the audience loved him. It was mostly Navy guys, and almost no women. I went up there. I had a suit and a tie, and I could just feel they hated me, right from the beginning. I opened up with a joke about how dogs use body language and when a dog shows you its belly it's saying, "Hey, I'm sorry I screwed up. Please come forgive me. Come on, look at my belly. I'm sorry." And there's more to the joke, but that's the basic premise. Well, 30 seconds into my act, some guy in the back yells, "You going to show us your belly when you're done?" Well, I'd been on stage like 45 seconds. I hadn't established any humor. Nobody was laughing. I didn't know what to do. I thought about using a stock line but I realized there are 300 people here. I can't just yell a stock line to the back of the room. I hadn't been funny. No one's going to take my side against his.

So what could I do? Well, if you're ever confused on stage, the old line is 'be honest'. As in life, honesty's usually the best policy. I didn't know what to do. I knew I couldn't use a line. I knew I wasn't going to run off stage crying. So I just looked out there and I said, "You know what? I've been on stage less than a minute." I said, "I know I haven't been funny." I said, "But they flew me out from Los Angeles to do a job. I've been doing the job all week. Give me a chance. Give me 5 minutes. If I'm not funny in 5 minutes, you let me know. I'll leave the stage and we'll bring the headlining act on." I said, "Does that sound fair?" And the audience applauded. I didn't know what else to do, but they sensed the honesty. They sensed the reality of the situation and all I was asking was a fair chance. And I got them on my side and started doing my regular routine, and was getting a better response than I normally would get.

After five or ten minutes, the heckler said something obnoxious again, And I gave him some good come-back lines, some stock ones. The audience was on my side, and they laughed and kind of made fun of him. And the rest of the show went great. Why? Because at that point, I was honest, I was able to establish credibility, and then I was able to put down the heckler.

Last thing I'll say about hecklers is this: don't be ashamed to leave the stage. There are times in your career where if you cannot get the job done because of hecklers, leave. I have seen the best comics in the country leave the stage. Jimmy Brogan, the head writer for the Tonight Show. I've seen Norm McDonald at the Improv leave the show. I've seen a ton of people leave the show. Rich Scheidner. Canyon Man. I've seen him walk off too. There's no shame in saying, "I can't do my job because you're heckling too much."

It happened to me once. Normally you don't want to leave the stage, but I finally said, "I can't do my job." If you ever feel you're in physical danger, get out. This is almost never going to happen. But again, I was in Santa Fe, New Mexico for a little rinky-dink two-nighter and there were 15 guys in the room. No women. They totally were drunk. Didn't like what I was talking about -- relationships. And maybe 15, 20 minutes into my set, just whoosh. Right past my head was a piece of ice. And I said, "Well, this show is officially over" and I challenged a guy to a fight, which was in hindsight, a big mistake. He didn't accept my challenge, but I should have just walked off. But if you ever feel like someone's throwing stuff at you, hey walk off. This is not the circus. This isn't the rodeo. People can't throw stuff at you. You know, there's that old thing, "Ah, we're going to throw tomatoes at you." No. I'm sorry. You can't throw stuff at the performers.

There was another time where a group of people right in front just wouldn't shut up. I'm having a good show and they won't shut up. Finally, I said, "I cannot get my jokes out." I go, "You have to be quiet." And so they said, "Shh." I'd try to continue, but they'd interfere every time. Every time. I asked them to leave. Nothing. I tried to get a bouncer to kick them out. Nothing. I finally said, "Look, we're going to take a vote." I said, "How many people" because I was headlining, "want the show to end right now? We go home and that's it. We call it a night." Nothing. No response. And I said,

"Now, how many think this guy and this group of guys at the table are a bunch of jerks and want them to get the hell out?" The place erupts. I look at the table and I say, "Well, democracy just spoke. See ya!" They didn't leave and they interrupted my next joke, and I looked around. I said, "Folks, there is nothing more I can do." I said, "I apologize. Come see a show later this week. I'll try to make sure you get in for free, but you can blame this table for what just happened. Good night." And I walked off.

The club owner actually apologized to me because he was not in the room, and they should have kicked them out. So again, establish credibility and 95% of the time that will shut the heckler up. That 2% to 3% of the time that you can't shut them up, get them kicked out. We'll talk about how to get them kicked out in a little bit. But if they don't get them kicked out and they keep talking, leave. There's no harm in that. There's no shame in that. You're there to do a job, and if someone is preventing you from doing that job, you have to leave or they have to leave. And if they won't, then you do.

7

<u>Anything Goes?</u>

When you're analyzing the audience, you want to think, "Is there anything that I cannot say to this audience? Is anything taboo?" Sometimes there is, If you're working in a certain state, like Utah. I work there in Provo quite often, and it is a Mormon town... 95% or 96% Mormon. The contract will come, and in it will be the provision that "There is no swearing. No references to God or Jesus," and that's fine. Those are the rules. Anything that you do is fine as long as you don't swear or make any references to God. So you can't say the "f" word there. That's taboo. Once I did a corporate show and asked "Is it okay if I say 'ass' because you can say it on TV?" They said "No, we don't want you use that word." Okay. You just have to ask, or you'll not know what's taboo.

Another thing that you want to think about is that if you're doing jokes that are edgy, think about what has happened in the news lately. Be cognizant of the world around you.

177

Comedy Career Management by **Barry Neal**

I was featuring in Phoenix and after I did my set I watched the headliner. He did a very funny joke about kidnapping a kid and he said stuff like, "Oh he threw up in the car. By the time I got him home there was pee everywhere. It stunk. It cost me hundreds of dollars to clean everything up. By the time I was done, it cost me $1000 to give the kid back." I'm not doing justice to the joke, but here's my point: he did the joke in Phoenix and nobody laughed the first night. As a matter of fact, people were not amused at all. I didn't know what was going on either. I was like, "Why are people like so taken aback?" Well, we found out. Two weeks prior there had been a child who was abducted and the result was a decapitated child. The moment he said words about kidnapping a kid, it triggered everyone's mind in the audience there in Phoenix. Now was that his fault? I think so. I think if you're going to do something that's a little on the edge, pushing the envelope, at least be aware of what's going on in the town that you're in.

I do a joke about school recess and how dangerous it is. We all remember recess. There's always some kid down at the bottom of the pile. "Get off. I can't breathe." It was crazy out there. My joke is like it's 10 minutes. You're sent outside. No rules. No adults. It's like a 10-minute version of 'Lord of the Flies'. Now that joke has always worked well for me. However, when Columbine happened and there was the terrible shooting outside the school, I totally took that joke out of my act for six months because I felt the moment I said recess and how dangerous it is and I'm shocked that nobody was hurt with what we did, I don't want to bring up memories of Columbine. So sometimes you have to just be a little bit aware and put some jokes away that may not be right. If you have an airline joke, don't do it right after an airline crash. Just use your common sense.

So if you're not sure if it's taboo, talk to the club owner. He'll know what's going on in the town. At least that way, you don't end up with 5 minutes of silence where people hate you.

8

Don't Blame Them

There will be times where you do a joke and the audience doesn't laugh. Again, there could be a lot of reasons why they don't laugh. One, they don't think it's funny. Two, something happened. You messed up a word. Three, a drink dropped. Four, a cell phone went off. A lot of things could have happened. The worst thing to do is blame the audience for not getting it.

I hate going to clubs where a comic does a joke, nobody laughs and they go, "Whoosh," as if to say, "Wow, that joke went over all your heads." Let's hypothetically say you're the smartest person I've ever met and that joke went over everyone's head. Now what? Now you've been just saying, "Not only did it go over your head, I think I'm smarter than everyone. You're all stupid." That's not going to win you any friends in that audience.

Problem number two is, it probably didn't go over everyone's head. I've been in the audience when a comic did that. I got

180

the joke. It wasn't funny to me. That's why I didn't laugh. So now, you're not only telling me I didn't laugh because I didn't get it, you're calling me stupid. I'm not stupid. I got the joke. It's not funny, and now I just think you're a jerk. So don't blame the audience for not getting it. If they don't get it, they don't get it. And if enough people don't get it, stop doing the joke, because it's probably just not funny.

9

Waiting For Applause

Now let's go to the flip side. You're doing jokes that are working real well. You're up there, you're cooking, you're in the zone. People are laughing and you get applause for it. Well that's when you do a joke and it's so clever, so good, and people go, "ha ha ha, oh... that's great." What you want to do is let them laugh. Let them applaud. Sometimes young comics, they're so excited that when they get the laughter, they don't know what to do and they just keep talking over the laughter. Let the audience laugh. If you run over them, they'll start thinking, "Maybe I shouldn't laugh. I should just wait" and then you'll never get a laugh. Timing is important.

The way it works is, take your time. Assume you're going to get a laugh. And then when you starting getting that little applause, go and maybe get a little drink of water. Let them go, "This is your time to applaud because that was well worth it." Glug glug glug. Put your drink down. What you want to do is let them applaud. Let that build up. That applause will build. Let it hit the top, the zenith of the applause and as it starts going down, then start your next line. Don't let it hit all the way to the bottom, because then you have to start up again. So let the applause build, get to the top, let it slide a little bit, and then pick it right up again.

So again, let the audience laugh. Let them applaud. They want to. If you take that away from them, they'll stop doing it completely.

10

Don't Talk To Them

When you're starting out, you should just emphasize material. It's a real danger to talk to the audience, because they're an 'X' factor. You really don't know what you're going to get. A lot of times you'll see experienced comics talk to the audience and they'll be able to riff with them and get a lot of laughter out of it. They really aren't riffing. They're doing prepared material because they know the general response they're going to get.

For example, I talk about relationships. If I see a man next to a woman, I'll say, "Is that your wife?" Well there's very few responses he can give. And then I'll ask, "How long have you been married?" A very pointed question. Now he could go a lot of ways. He could say, "Six years." He could say, "Uhh" and look at her. He could say, "Uhh, ask her." There are a lot of different boxes that he could check off. Either way, I have a joke. If he says "Six years", I'll just say, "Is he right? Congratulations, you're one of the few men that who knows how

184

long he's been married." That gets a laugh. If he looks at her, I'll say, "Don't look at her. What are you, whipped? What? You can't answer for yourself? I'm talking to you, tough guy." That gets a big laugh. Or if he's wrong, if he says seven and she says six, I'll say, "Oh great. We have a winner of the *who's not getting any tonight* contest."

My point is this, most questions that you will see comics ask an audience, we already know the answer. Or if we don't know the answer, there's only like four or five boxes that they can choose from. And in every box I have an answer, and it looks like it's off the cuff, but it's not. I've done it for years. I've heard every response. So although it looks like I'm riffing, I'm not.

So my advice to you is that if you start talking to the audience and you're not ready, if you don't know all of the responses you might get, you're in trouble. I worked a club one time when I was starting out and I was struggling. It was some bar and the layout of the room was so that the audience was in front of me. Off to the side, they were watching the Lakers game. Like most young comics, I felt, "Wow. My material's not working. I better just talk to the audience. Maybe that'll help." I looked over and said, "Hey, how are the Lakers doing?" and I heard a voice say, "Better than you." My set was effectively over, because he was right.

An audience can sink you faster than an iceberg did the Titanic. You will not get help from the audience. If the audience senses you are struggling, they sense you are out of control; they sense you may not be a captain, so you certainly, if you're losing control, you don't want to say, "Ahh, you be the captain." You've got to get your wits together and bring that focus back. Bring that control back and say, "I am in control. I will make you laugh."

Don't ask the audience open-ended questions, because you're always going to get a response that you're not expecting. I see comics do this all the time. "Hey, what do you do for a living?" There could be a thousand answers. What the comic is hoping for is somebody will say, "Nothing" and then they have a response for that, like "oh, you work for the government." Or "how do you know when you're done?" Great. But what if they don't say it, "I do nothing." What if they say, "I'm an accountant"? What if they say, "I'm a computer con- sultant"? I've seen people do that. "I've got nothing for that." You're just wasting time. If you have to talk to the audience, if you feel you want to interact, fine. Just ask them pointed questions so that you'll get a specific answer. You only have to answer one of two ways. "Are you married?" Yes or no. That's it. Maybe they're engaged.

Be careful. You think the audience is your friend and they're there to help you. They're not. They're there to sit back, relax and listen to you. So please don't send the anchor out and say, "Help. Help me. I'm stranded. Help me, audience." They won't. They will eat you alive, like sharks.

11

<u>Energy Crisis</u>

When you start out doing comedy, the crowds aren't going to be very large. You may be working in front of anywhere from four people to 40 people. If you're thinking "Four people. How can I do it?" Well, you know what? I've done it and I've had good shows.

Don't blame the four people that are there for the other 200 that aren't. Don't give less energy to them. Now granted, you can't sit there and make a big production and be really loud because the room is small. There's only four people, but you still have to give them a quality show. If there's 12 people, give them a show. Don't sit there in a huff and puff and just say, "Well, there's 12 people. I guess you get my B material."

Hey, these people paid to see your show. Be a professional. Give them your best. Don't blame the audience, the one that is there, for the one that is not.

12

Parties In The House?

As a comic, you want to get there before the show starts not only to tell the MC and the owner that you're there. To me it's important to watch the whole show. I watch the comics in front of me because I get to see what's going on. I get to know who's in the audience. Is there a birthday party, or for me even better, like a bachelor or bachelorette party? When I know they're in the room, I can walk out on stage and appear as though I am very knowledgeable. You want to appear almost omniscient to these people. "Wow! How does he know that there's a birthday party?" Why? Because I was watching. I know who's heckling. I know who the person they picked on in the front row is. I know that in the front row there's a cop with his girlfriend. I watch the show completely before I go on, so I know who I can pick on, where the laughter's coming from, who maybe is a possible heckler, where the birthday parties are, and this will help you quell any riots that happen during your show.

Here's an example. I was in San Jose and there was a birthday party for Bob. He brought five of his buddies and they were kind of loud and boisterous. The MC went up, and as an MC has to do, asks "Hey, are there any parties? Any birthdays?" And Bob goes, "Whoo! It's my birthday! Blah blah blah." And very soon, Bob was heckling and his whole party was heckling, and the opening act didn't really know how to handle it and within five to seven minutes, it was clear he lost control of the room to Bob and his posse. He left the stage.

The second guy comes up and he tries to become friends with Bob. "Hey Bob. I like you. Happy birthday" and he tries to suck up and it works a little bit. And he does his show and he gets a few laughs. But Bob and his people keep heckling. And the comic just turned on Bob, "Shut up! I'm trying to do a show! Blah blah blah." And he lost control. He lost his temper. He lost his control. He didn't have the audience really on his side and all of a sudden, there was anarchy. He lost the room.

So I thought to myself, "Okay, I've seen the show for 45 minutes. Bob and his posse of five or six friends are ruining this show. I need to take matters into my own hands." So I get introduced, "Ladies and gentlemen, Barry Neal." I grab the microphone and instead of going into my bit, I say, 'Thank you very much." I then add, "Bob, I know it's your birthday. On behalf of everyone in the audience, we'd like to say happy birthday - and shut the 'F' up." I didn't say 'F'. I said the word. And the audience went crazy and even Bob and his posse were like "Woo hoo."

Audiences are a little like children. They need to be disciplined sometimes and when I showed that I was in charge and that I was willing to discipline them, they shut up. They realized 'I'm not going to let you ruin the show. You may screw around with the other two guys. You're not doing it on my time,' and they shut up and they listened.

So again, watch the people who go on before you. If you don't, you can look very, very stupid. Believe me. I was at the Improv a lot and I would see people just show up maybe a few minutes before their time, pop up on stage and ask the same question over and over.

One time there was a cop in the audience and he was with a girl, and the first guy that said it, it was funny. Guy says, "I'm a cop." And the comic says, "Yeah. And who's that? Your hooker?" It got a big laugh from the audience. Ha ha ha ha. Cop and a hooker. Ha ha ha.

Well, about an hour later, some other comic came onstage who wasn't watching the show, starts riffing with the audience and he says to this guy, "What do you do?" Guy says, "Oh, I'm a cop." Comic says, "Hey, what's that? A hooker?" And nobody was laughing. Everyone was like, "We've already heard that joke."

And believe it or not, 30 minutes later another comic came up on stage, saw the guy, because he was a big guy in the front row, he goes, "Wow, you're a big guy. What do you do for a living?" Literally, audience members were screaming, "He's a cop." And boy that guy was so embarrassed and his show was almost ruined because the audience was like, "How do we know more than you do?" You never want that. When you're analyzing the audience you should be on top of things. You should be the one knowing everything that's going on. If you appear more knowledgeable than anyone in the room, again, they won't question your authority.

But that third comic that had to ask, how could you not question his authority? How can you be a great stand-up and not know he's a cop? There are 200 people. We all know he's a cop. How do you not know? You know why? Because he didn't watch what was going on before. And when you analyze the audience, the best thing you could do is get there early. Watch the show. Watch how it develops.

13

Are They There For Dancing?

Quite often when starting out, you'll be working in places that aren't full time comedy clubs. Maybe it's a bar or some other type of place has comedy from 8 to 10, but at 10 to 12, they have dancing. So right after comedy is done, dancing is there. I always like to know who's in the audience. Are they there for comedy or are they there for dancing? If they're showing up for comedy, great. I try to act as if it's a real audience in a real comedy club.

But there are times when you have to recognize that they're not. There's a club in Idaho that features comedy from 8 o'clock to 10 o'clock. Starting at 10 o'clock they do dancing. Well when the show starts late, as it inevitably does, if I'm the headliner, I'm on stage and at 9:30 people are beginning to walk into the room. They're walking in and they see this comedian, and they're talking because they don't care that I'm on stage. And I know they're not there for the comedy show, because my show's about to end in 10 minutes. They're there to dance, and to get ready to dance, and to drink before the dance. So as long as I know that, I give them more of a leash. I don't expect them to sit attentively.

All I can say is sometimes when they are not in the room to listen to comedy, maybe they're there just to drink at the bar and not watch, you have to have a longer leash and not say, "You're heckling me." They're not. They just don't care.

14

Did They Get In Free?

Another thing I like to find out in a club is if the audience got in free, because if they got in free, I feel as though I have to give them a bigger leash to be rowdy. Not that I want them to be rowdy, but the fact is, there's a perceived value in the show. If you go to a show for free, the perceived value is 'how good can it be?' If someone told me, "I'm going to see this play and it's $30". I'd say, "Well, okay. I'm going to expect to see a darn good play." If someone says, "Oh you're going to see a play." "How much is it?" "Oh, it's free". My expectations are going to be a lot lower and quite frankly if I walk out, I walk out. Why? First of all, there's no perceived value.

Second, there's no investment in the show. If people get in free and they get drunk and they heckle and they get kicked out, whoopidee doo. I didn't put any money into the show. I just bought drinks. However, you do a show and you charge 15 bucks at the door a head, well all of a sudden now you've got a guy and his date. They've already shelled out $30 just to sit down. It's a real good chance, they're not going to be apt to get drunk and heckle and get kicked out, because they already have an investment in the show. So that's always something I like to find out. Who are these people? Are they there for a party? Are they there to dance? Did they get in free?

15

Crowd Control

I discussed hecklers earlier. One of the things when dealing with hecklers is I want to know how I can control them. I find out is the room controlled. What that means is, is there a bouncer or bouncers that will kick these people out if I ask for it. If there is not, again, I have to give a longer leash and say, "There's no one who's going to kick them out, so I have to put up with a little more heckling because my only other alternative is to leave." And that's always a last resort.

If the room is controlled, and they say, "Yeah, we have people", what I like to do is go up to the bouncer and say, "Listen. I never have a problem with hecklers, because I rarely do. Maybe once a year. Maybe twice. But if I'm having a problem with a table, I will give you a cue." Sometimes a cue can be "Hey, can I buy this guy a drink?" or "Can I get another glass of water up here?" That's a verbal cue to the person who wants to kick the heckler out, the bouncer or the manager, to get them out because you don't want to sit there and say, "You know what? You have to leave now" because you don't want to be the bad guy being the comic. There are times that I've done that. But more often than not, I just like to use a verbal cue to the bouncer and say, "You know what? I think I'd like to buy this guy a drink." The bouncer comes over and kicks the guy out. It's nice to have that authority.

We talked about being a headliner and some people think it's a tough position. I personally think it's the easiest position because I have that authority to kick people out. When I was a feature, it's tough for me to say, "Hey, you know what? You have to leave," because quite frankly the headliner is the star. So now that I'm the last guy up, I look at people and say, "You know what? If you don't think I'm funny, it's really time to go because show's over after me." So that's another thing that I use against the heckler. I'll say, "Ya' know what? If you don't think I'm funny, it's really time to go because there ain't nothing else happening after I'm on stage."

So again, find out who's in charge of bouncing the people, get to know them, become friends with them and then maybe give them a verbal cue so they can take care of any unwanted business.

16

Call Backs

When I'm in the middle of my show, I always want to make sure the audience is listening and paying attention. And again, you can analyze the audience by a lot of things, like their body movements. If they're wrapped up with their arms crossed, they're probably not happy. And if they're yawning or looking at their watch, these are things to notice. So when I do a joke that I'm going to call back later, it's imperative that they get the joke the first time I say it.

Most movies have call backs, like a signature line that warrants being used again. Whether it's a drama or a comedy, there's going to be a call back. Clint Eastwood's *Dirty Harry* movies are famous. They've had shirts made. In the first *Dirty Harry* movie he made, remember this call back... "Do you feel lucky? Well do you punk?" It's a great line. It's a line that was said by hundreds of thousands of kids all over. If you've never seen the movie, real briefly, very first scene in the movie, there's a robbery. Dirty Harry takes care of it, shoots one of the guys. The robber is sitting next to a gun. Dirty Harry comes up. He goes, "Ah ah ah. I know what you're thinking. Did he fire six shots or only five? Well to tell you the truth, in all this excitement, I've kind of lost track myself. But seeing this is a .44 magnum, the most powerful handgun in the world, and could blow your head clean off, you've got to ask yourself one question. 'Do I feel lucky?' Well do ya', punk?" And in that scene, we look at the robber and he looks at the gun and he's about to go for it and then he decides 'I'm not sure. I'm not going to take that chance.' And his hand goes down and he surrenders. And if you remember the movie, Dirty Harry comes up He goes "click". He had fired all six shots.

Now that was a great scene unto itself, but what made the movie really great is it gets called back at the end. Very end of the movie, he's chasing the villain. I think Scorpio was his name, and he shoots him in the leg. Sure enough, Scorpio falls down. The gun is right next to him. Dirty Harry has the gun and he goes, "Ah ah ah" and he says the same exact line. "I know what you're thinking. Did I fire six shots or five? Well do you feel lucky? Well do ya' punk?" And sure enough, just as a classic movie is, this time the bad guy goes for the gun to go to shoot Dirty Harry, not knowing that Harry had one bullet left. He shoots the bad guy... end of movie.

It started at one place. It ended in one place. It was call-back. It puts a little ribbon on the movie. And that's what call-backs do in your act. You say something and it's funny, then you call it back and it puts a little ribbon on the joke. Every one of my TV spots, I have always ended with a call back. It's a sure fire laugh getter because if they liked it the first time, they're going to love it the second time. Every comedy has a call-back. Almost every comedy will be calling something back, whether it's a phrase, or whether it's a scene or something that had to do with something that was magical.

Have you seen Adam Sandler in The *Waterboy*? In one scene, he's showing his girlfriend a special water that he has in his room. At the time you're thinking, "What does this scene mean? Why are we seeing this so-called special water?" Well, it's important because it's going to be called back. At the very end of the movie, Adam Sandler is hit and he's hurt, and it doesn't look like he can get up and play, and he needs water but not just any water. So his girlfriend goes and gets that special water, Adam Sandler drinks it. We know, as the audience, what that water means. Had we come in after that scene, we wouldn't have gotten it. And had that scene not been in there, it wouldn't have made sense that there was all of a sudden special water, so it was a set up.

We set something up and we call it back later. All comedies have it. All great movies have it. All great comedians have it. They call back stuff. It wraps it around really nicely, puts a little bow on it, and presents it to the audience.

17

Similar Material

Often you'll be doing shows where there are 10 to 15 comics on the bill. Again, I like to get there early to make sure no one is doing very similar material to me. If there are 10 or 15 comics, sometimes there'll be people doing, like let's say Catholic school bits. Well, it's important that if someone did a Catholic school bit and you have a Catholic school bit, all you need to do is say, "Well, you know, Gene was talking about going to Catholic school. Well, when I went to Catholic school, here's what I thought." That's all you need to do because if you don't reference that, the audience will think, "Aw, we already heard a Catholic school bit. We don't want to hear another one."

If three or four people are also doing Catholic school bits, maybe you ought to want to drop yours if you're following them. So again, watch the people who are in front of you and try not to duplicate material that's been done too many times.

18

Celestine Prophecy

I Recently read a book titled *The Celestine Prophecy'* and found it very interesting, so I recommend you that read it too. One of the chapters in it is *Interaction.* And I say this because again, the relationship that the audience has with the performer, is very interesting because it's tied into what the book was talking about.

There are times in relationships, where some people are in control and other people are submissive, and that's what you want to build. You want to, at times, just submit your own will, bring your defenses down and go, "You know what? You make the decisions." And we've all been like that at times. "You know what? I trust you. Because I trust you I will let my guard down. I will submit my will to you and you lead the way." And that's what you want from the audience. You want to get them and get them strong in the beginning and tell them, "I am in control. Trust me. I will be funny." And the audience because they are the audience, they want that. They want to be led. They need a leader. They will eventually let down their defenses and they will let you impose your will on them. And they will submit because they trust you. And that is magic when you have the room in your hand and you can lead them anywhere you want and you can feel it. You've got to start strong to do that though. And that's when you have complete control of the room. Their will is yours. Take it and guide them. They want to be led.

19

No Mingling

I'm a firm believer that when we're dealing with the audience, we do not mingle with them before the show. Why? Because the audience should see you as a star. You don't want the audience seeing you before the show, drinking a beer right next to them. You're not one of them. You're not their peer. You're the star. That's why green rooms were invented. Green rooms separate the celebrities from the audience. And I'm not saying we're better than they are, but you want that image of 'the first time you see me is the lights are on me and I have a microphone' and you're bigger than life. That's why people are attracted to celebrities because it's almost a bigger than life thing. You don't want them to know that you were the guy in the bathroom, puking because you had too many beers. You don't want that. Do that in the green room. If you're going to do that after the show, fine. But it's important that their first view of you is, "Oh! Wow! Look at them! They're on a stage. They have lights."

Here's an example. When I was in college, I saw 'West Side Story' and thought the girl who played Maria was beautiful. She was short, dark hair, very exotic, great body and I was thinking, "Wow, do I want to meet her." I knew a lot of the people in the crew so I said, "You know, if you guys are all going out afterwards, I'd love to hang out with you guys and get to meet Maria." They said, "Sure. We're all going to out to the bars." I said, "Great." So we went out and I got to hook up with her, and I talked with her for almost 20 minutes. She swore. She drank. She had tattoos. She was ready to do drugs. I'm not saying these are bad things, but just not right for me. And I just totally was just like, "Ah, this is so not the right person for me."

My point is this, had I gone out with her before I saw her in the show, it would have changed the whole show for me. I would have been watching the show going, "Hmm. Boy. Now that I know her, it's hard for me to look at her as Maria" and you don't want that. You don't want people seeing you before the show saying, "Yeah. Boy. My car lost a muffler and my girlfriend dumped me and I'm drinking beer and I'm a loser" or whatever your bad day is. You want them to look at you like you're a star.

Don't mingle. Don't hang out with the crowd before the show. If you want to hang out afterwards, that's fine because they're going to look at you very differently then. They're going to want to hang out with you. They're going to want to buy you drinks. They're going to want to talk to you. They're going to want to be your friend. Before the show, you're nobody. You're almost like one of them. So don't hang out before the show and mingle with the crowd. It's not appropriate.

20

<u>Knowledge Is Power</u>

In conclusion, the more you know about the audience, the better. That's why I say go to the show early. Watch all the comics that go onstage before you. Watch what they do. See where the laughter's coming from. Find out who the hecklers are.

I'll give you an example. Say I was to go out on a blind date with a girl, and I got a portfolio on her that said she loves sushi, she likes relationship movies, and she likes Rocky Road ice cream. Well I guarantee you, when we went out, I'd say, "Hey, you know what? I'd love to go to a sushi restaurant. What do you think?" And we'd go. And I'd say, "You know what? There's a new Meg Ryan film playing. I'd like to see it. Let's go." Then at the end maybe we'd go for a walk and I'd spy an ice cream parlor, and

I'd go, "Oh, you know what? I'd love to share some ice cream. I like Rocky Road. How about it?" I'm not guaranteeing that we're going to hook up that night but there's a really good chance I'm going to get to see her again. Why? Because I knew a lot about her in advance. It's almost like the movie 'Groundhog Day' where Bill Murray knew things about Andie McDowell. You can press the right buttons. The more you know about the audience, the more buttons you can press to make sure they like you.

SECTION IV:
PERFORMANCE
&
SURROUNDINGS

1

<u>Introduction</u>

In this Fourth Section, we'll be discussing performance and the surroundings of a stand-up comedy venue. Tips that we're going to give to you that will help improve your performance during a show.

There are a lot of things that people not in the business don't realize we have to take into consideration, and in this particular Section we'll be covering several of them.

You'll be learning what is important and how to deal with things like the room's lighting, the general surroundings, the all-important microphone, and the general layout of the room. All things that a real pro takes into consideration and that the general public never even thinks about.

Comedy is a serious business, and in this Section you'll be learning that it takes more than just getting up there and being funny.

2

<u>Going Blank</u>

Let's say that you're performing and you forget your set. You lose your mental place. You think, "Oh my goodness. I'm in the middle of my set and I don't remember the next joke." Relax. One of the things that can help you from blanking is to think about it in terms of themes. Go into it with a preparation in terms of, "Okay the first three minutes is going to be about my family, and I have these seven jokes. The next four minutes is on my job and I have these 10 jokes. And the last will be about my relationship, with these eight jokes." So if you have three themes, you're never going to get that lost.

And if you're doing stuff about your job and can't remember the 6th or 7th joke, don't worry. Nobody in the audience has your script. Nobody's going to say, "Wait a minute! He missed the sixth or the seventh joke!" Don't worry about it. If you blank or forget where you're at, just move on. So forget the rest of the job jokes, move on to the relationship jokes. So keep it in terms of themes.

There are a lot of times I'm doing 60 minutes and I may not remember a joke. It's okay. You move on. People don't have your script. We think they do, but they don't. So as long as you don't act like, "Oh my gosh, I'm lost." Take a second. Get a drink of water. No one's going to say, "Wait, he's getting a drink of water because he's lost." As a comic, I may pick up on it but as an audience member, they never do.

I'll give you an example. We talked about call backs in the last series. I end my show with a call back. One of the jokes at the very end is, "It's hard to win an argument with my wife because I can never ask her what's wrong because if you ever ask a woman she'll always say, 'Well if you don't know'" and I throw my hands up and I walk away. And that always gets a laugh, "Well if you don't know!" And I end my show with—I do that joke and then I do like three or four minutes and then my show closes with, "It's very difficult because sometimes after we're intimate my wife will ask me what I'm thinking about and I don't want to say sports, and I can't lie, but I can't tell her the truth. I figured out the perfect response. Every time she snuggles up next to me and asks me, 'What are you thinking about?' I just look at her and say, "Well if you don't know!" And boom. Huge laugh, applause. "Thank you, I'm out of here. My name is Barry Neal. Good night!"

Once I actually forgot to do the beginning set-up part of the "Well if you don't know!" call-back, and about two sentences before I knew I was going to end my set, I kept thinking, "Oh no. I didn't set up the end joke, but I closed with it anyway. I just went along with "Every time she snuggles up and says 'What are you thinking?' I just said, "Well if you don't know" and still got a laugh because I sold it. It didn't get nearly the response normally it would have if I had remembered to set it up properly, but nobody in the audience was thinking, "Wait a minute. Had he set that joke up earlier, then it would have killed." Nobody knows, so don't worry about blanking.

Don't acknowledge it unless it's so obvious that you have to just say, "Folks, this is only my third time on stage. I forgot my act. Let's go to the cheat sheet." That's a last resort. You really don't want to do that.

3

<u>Dying On Stage</u>

When you're starting out and the show is not going well it's called *dying on stage*. We use that term because it feels like death. If you're not doing well, don't acknowledge it. Smile. Have a good time. Laugh. Act as if things are going great. This is exactly the response I want because a lot of the times, the audience has no idea that you're dying.

On more than one occasion people have come up and said, "Boy did we love that show" and I'm thinking, "Boy did you not let me know during the show." They weren't laughing. Some audiences aren't laughers. They're smiling. They're nodding. They're appreciating. The last thing I want to tell them is, "I'm dying" because now it puts in their mind, "Oh. Maybe he is dying. Maybe he's not doing well at all. Maybe he's not that funny." Again, it's authority and control you are losing if you admit that you are dying.

There will be some times when you're obviously not doing well. It's obvious to you.

It's obvious to them. It's obvious to anyone who's watching, that you're not doing well. So what do you do? I never admit that I'm dying because I don't feel as though it's my fault. Maybe that's egotistical, but I don't. What I feel is that it's not a good match. There's a relationship between me and the audience, and tonight we're just not mixing. Again, it's like a date.

We've all been on dates where you sit there and within 15 minutes, it's like, "Boy, this date's going nowhere." It's not her fault. It's not your fault. It's just not a good match. And then at that point you could admit that to the audience. Just say, "You know what folks? If you as an audience and me as a performer ever think about getting back together, let's not." And at least the audience can laugh and appreciate the fact that you acknowledge the situation, you're trying to do the best you can, and for some reason unbeknownst to everyone, it's not going well. It's not their fault. They don't suck as an audience. And it's not your fault. You don't suck as a performer. You just aren't a good match together. And that's okay.

4

A Tough Act To Follow

One of the hardest things to do in stand-up when you're performing is following someone who did very well. You may think, "Oh, isn't that good? The guy in front of me did well. The audience is all ready and primed?" Actually, you want the person in front of you to do well, but not that well. Here's the reason: the audience always feels as though it's a competition. It's not, but the audience feels that way. So when the person who is on stage before you leaves, they feel as though the next performer has forced them off the stage even though that's not the case. So if you're following someone who's tough, the audience thinks, "Boy we sure did like that last person. Are you as funny as they are?"

It's a very tough situation to be in. So here's the problem. What are you going to do when you have to follow someone who's tough? Yes, you've got a problem on your hands. What I'd like to say is this: try to get someone to do time in between you to sort of be the buffer between you. And that's the job of the MC. They take one for the team. They take a bullet for the team, so to speak. So if someone just killed in front of me, I push the MC and say, "go do five minutes. Have them hate you."

And that was my job at the Improv. Usually, 95% of the people are great there, so their closing bit kills and people would go, "Whoo!" then I would go up and do a few minutes and bring the audience back down. Otherwise, what happens is the audience is way up there because they've had a great time. If I bring someone right up, you can't match that audience's expectations. It's hard to jump right up, so you're down here starting out and the audience is up here. So the job of the MC is to do some time, so that the audience comes back down. And now all of a sudden when I introduce you, you're on a level ready for the audience to laugh with.

Basically, I'm getting them to hate me; for them to go, "Ugh. Gosh. We can't wait for the next performer." And then I bring you up and you look great. So again, if you're following a tough act, have the MC do some time. It really makes your job a lot easier.

Now let's say you're in a time crunch and you don't have time for the MC to do material or the MC is out of material. What are you going to do? Most important is let the audience know it is not a competition, so what I'll do is I'll say, "Hey, how about a hand for Joe. He was great." And I'll start applauding for myself. It shows that I'm gracious. It shows "Hey, it's not a competition. I want you guys to know I thought Joe was great. Yay!" And I'll let the audience applaud themselves out for Joe and then it'll kind of bring them down and go, "Oh. All right. Now we can listen to this guy." I'm not trying to win them over right away. I'm not trying to run out and go, "Forget Joe. It's me!" because that's not going to work. Let them applaud for Joe. Joe was great. Good for Joe. Now it's my turn.

I'd always rather follow someone that bombed. Some people don't understand that, but believe me, if I follow someone that bombs, the audience's expectations are way down and they can't wait to see someone funny. So when I take the stage, and I say the first funny thing, they're like,

"Oh, thank you! We love you." But you're not always going to follow someone who bombs. So if you can't, and you're following a killer, either have someone do time as a buffer or acknowledge how great they were and bring the audience in on how gracious you are, so then you can begin.

5

<u>Cutting It Short</u>

Okay, now we're working professionally and we're up on stage. There are times when you are going to be given a light. The audience normally will not be able to see the light. It'll be in front of you but it will be high up and the audience won't be able to see it. So when that light goes on, that's an indicator that you have a certain amount of time to get off stage. You have to know how to cut your act to get off stage. Most of the time you'll be given what's called a five-minute light. That means you have five minutes to get off. When you see the light, normally it's a red light, all you have to do is hold the microphone and just gently nod. The audience doesn't know why you're nodding and they don't even realize that you are. But just it's a nod that says, "I see the light. I know what I'm doing." Now if you're only doing a 10-minute set, you'll probably get a one-minute or a two-minute light. There's no reason for a five-minute light in a 10-minute set.

So how do you cut your act? Here's what you want to do? You must time out every segment of your act. Figure out how long your closing bit is. My closing bit is three minutes, so I want a five-minute light. If I'm doing a 45-minute set, give me a five-minute light. But wait, your closing bit is only three minutes. Why do you need a five-minute light? Well, if I get a five-minute light, and I'm in the middle of my set somewhere, I see the light. I now have two minutes left to get from where I am, finish my joke, maybe do another joke and then do my last three minutes. I need those two minutes as a buffer to get me from where I am to smoothly transition to my last three minutes.

So if your last joke or bit is a minute, get a two-minute light. That way when you see the light, you've given yourself one minute to finish whatever joke you're in, smoothly transition to start your last minute bits.

You have to know your material inside and out. You have to know how long each bit is. If you're doing a 10-minute set, quite frankly, you shouldn't need a watch. Really, I don't need a watch on stage. I have one, but I almost never need to look. If you were to tell me, "Hey tell me where you are at the 34-minute mark." I'll tell you right now, I wouldn't be off by more than a joke. I know my set so well inside and out that I know where I'm at. You have to know your set so well that you can go forwards, backwards, if someone says, "Hey, start in the middle and go this way or go that way", that's the way you need to do it. Again, it's a business. It's not just magic that people are laughing. They're doing it because you need to know your stuff inside and out. So if people say 'cut your act', you have to know how to cut and when to cut.

More importantly, you need to make sure you're not cutting something very important. Let's say someone says, "Hey, instead of doing 20, do 10." You're thinking, "Oh, well I can't. I've already -- I've prepared my 20. That's it. I have to do 20." No, you have to do 10. So cut out 10 minutes but make sure if you cut out 10 minutes, if you're going to end with a big call back, don't cut out that first time that you do the joke, so it makes sense when you call it back. You see what I'm saying? Set the joke up, keep it in as a call back. So don't cut that part.

I was doing a show with Rita Rudner in San Diego. Beautiful five star hotel they put us in. My wife and I had a great time. But here's how well I had to cut my act.

They told me, "Prepare to do 30 minutes." So I got there. It was a huge amphitheater. Thirty minutes, no problem. Well, about 10 minutes before the show, they tell me, "Rita has to catch a plane. Do 20 minutes." I said, "Okay, I'll do 20 minutes." So I'm thinking, "All right, what am I going to cut? What am I going to cut? Good. I got it. Twenty minutes." I am being introduced. I see Rita come out of her dressing room and one of her managers runs up to me as the introduction is being done and says, "Psst, Rita wants you to do 10." I'm not even given 10 seconds to prepare for that.

So as I'm walking from backstage to the microphone, I'm thinking, "20 to 10. Twenty to 10. What am I going to cut?" and that's how well you need to know your set. I had to cut my set in half, keep all my call backs, keep my beginning strong, keep my end strong and everything in the middle that worked and make it ten. And it worked. It went great. As a matter of fact at the nine-minute mark, I saw Rita who was in the back. She came out of the dressing room looking at her watch and I know what she was doing. I was very much on time. I think I finished in 10 minutes and 10 seconds, got off stage, said "Thank you very much" and Rita came in and just knocked them dead. She did a great job. So you need to know how to cut your set. If someone says, "Do 20" and then they say, "Do 10", you can't say, "No, I can't!" You have to cut. When that red light goes on, signal with a nod and make sure you get off stage in whatever time you said you would get off. If it was a 3-minute light, get off in 3. If it was a 5-minute light, get off in 5.

If it flashes consistently, that means 'get off now'. For whatever reason you can't figure out, if the red light is constantly flashing, that means, "Get off now. We're going to have a talk after you're done."

You can request the kind of light that you want in terms of do you want a 3-minute light, or a 5-minute light or a 2-minute light. Again, the important part is knowing how long your last bit is. If your last bit is 2 minutes, don't get a 2-minute light. Give yourself at least a 3-minute light so you have that last minute to swing to the last 2 minutes.

In my headlining set I want a 5-minute light. So I have 5 minutes, I see the light. I need my 3 minutes, so I get 2 minutes to get from 5 to the last 3 minutes. There's a little bit of math involved. But again, if I get a 5-minute light, I finish up my joke. I have 2 minutes to do whatever I have to do to get to my last bit, which is 3 minutes long.

Earlier we covered not going over your time, but I'll tell you how important it is to cut your time when you're asked. I was working in Vegas as an opening act, and I was very nervous because this was my first time in Vegas and I wanted to please. The show was supposed to run from eight to nine. Well, I'm supposed to do 15 minutes. I did my 15 minutes and I thought I did my time and everything's fine. The headliner did 46 instead of doing 45. Then I had to come out to finish up in 30 seconds, go "Thank you very much. We have a great show next week. Blah blah blah. Good night."

The show ran two minutes over. Two minutes over. It ended at 9:02. I mean I didn't even think of it. I didn't even know it ended at 9:02. I figured '9:02, it's perfect. We're right on time. It's within schedule. That's within that 10% leeway. We're fine. Sixty-minute show, you have a 6 minute leeway.'

Not in Vegas. When that light goes on for the headliner in Vegas, get off now. I had three guys in suits who were not kidding around when they cornered me in the green room and they said, "You know what time it is?" "9 o'clock?" "It's 9:02." "Okay." And they said, "You know what that means?" And I'm thinking, "I hope it means I don't get whacked." They said, "Every minute that people are in this room and not in the casino, we are losing x amount." It was like thousands of dollars. And he said, "We blame you. You just cost us like $20,000 by it running over two minutes." And I'm thinking, "I'm not making $20,000."

So, when someone says cut your time, they're doing it for a reason. You better be able to cut your time. Believe me, the next day, I went up to the guy, the headliner and I said, "Psst," I said, "At 8:59, you have to be off stage." And he said, "Why?" And I told him the story. And I said, "I'm serious. Because at 8:59 and 30 seconds, I'm walking out and taking the microphone and saying, 'Goodbye' because I don't want these guys talking to me anymore." So when someone says, "Make sure you see the light and get off stage", it's there for a reason.

6

Slow Down and Annunciate

Another performing tip for young comics is to slow down. Some people have a natural slow pace and that's great. But most comics, myself included, when I started out, and even sometimes now, get so excited. I get so energized that I talk too fast. And when you talk too fast, you lose the annunciation.

When you're on stage, everything in your body is speeding up. Everything is telling you to go faster and faster, but unfortunately that's the exact opposite of what you really need to do. You want to slow it down. Control yourself. You can be manic but be in control.

Think about a salesman. Are you going to trust a salesman who's talking too fast like Joe Isuzu? No, you don't want a guy "bup bup bup bup bup bup bup." Relax. Slow down. You're going too fast.

You're scaring me." Be in control. If you're in control, you're slowing down, you're annunciating. Again, the control, the authority, clearly you have it because you're willing to take your time and annunciate. If they can't hear you, they can't laugh. If you're going too fast, you're going to run over their laughs. Slow it down. Watch yourself on tape. Sometimes I watch myself and I say, "Wow, I am going way too fast. I'm going on that 33 rpm. I'm going way too fast." So slow down. Annunciate. Take your time. The audience isn't going anywhere.

7

Inserting New Material

So you're growing as a performer. You have your plan. You're focused. You're working hard. You're trying out new material because you're writing every day. Great. Where are you going to put that new material? Well here are two places you don't want to put the new material. You never put new material in the beginning. Why? Because again, you have to establish your credibility. You have to come out strong. And if you come out strong in the first three minutes, the audience is going to relax. Remember their defense mechanisms? They'll go away. They'll submit their will and they'll let you be funny. So start out strong. You also want to end strong. If you end weak, people will always remember the ending. You want to end like gangbusters where people are, "Waaaaah!" Always the new stuff in the middle. People will forgive what's in the middle.

Again, think about movies. If a movie starts out with 10 minutes and it's a shoot 'em up movie and it's a great, exciting opening, you're going to watch for at least another 30 minutes. Even if the middle lags, you're going to let it go because you're like, "Wow, that opening was great." And then if that ending is just a kick ass ending, it's like, "Wow! What fireworks! What excitement! What drama!" You're going to go, "You know, that movie was pretty good." Even though for like 40 minutes in the middle, it dragged a little bit but boy, the ending was cool. Start strong. End strong. Weakness in the middle its almost always forgiven.

I was headlining in Houston and a girl was featuring or was showcasing. She came in. She wasn't the normal feature. The normal feature couldn't make it that night so there was a girl who said, "I'll come in, do 30 minutes and kind of showcase, and if you like what I do, you can hire me." And I'm headlining and I watch the girl, see how funny she is, see what she does with the audience. She came out and in five minutes and was killing them. I was thinking, "Wow. This is very good. I'm going to have trouble following this." She does the next 20 minutes. It was so bad, I could have sworn tumbleweeds were going by. You could hear crickets. I'm thinking, "This is really awful. She only had five minutes." Well, the last five minutes, in her defense, she picked it up and just had a really, really great ending like the last three to four just really got an applause break at the end. She said, "Thank you very much." I thought, "Well, she had 10 minutes." I did my show. Everything went fine.

Afterwards she comes up. She's all excited. I said, "Wow. Congratulations. You really did good" thinking, "Eh, you didn't do that good but I'm being gracious." She said, "I just got booked to feature." And I'm thinking, "You got booked here after they just saw that set?" You know what? What they saw was the beginning. What they saw was the people at the end loving her. Everything in the middle, got forgotten because people remember the ending. And you'll only make it to that ending if you start strong.

So again, come out strong. In the middle, hang in there, do your stuff. If you want to try out new material, hopefully, it's all strong. But if you have to be weak, be weak in the middle and close it strong.

That's again a baseball analogy. You have good starting pitching and you have a closer that closes every game. Your middle relief may not be the strongest, but as long as you can start strong and you can close it, you're fine. You're going to win a lot of pennants. In comedy, it's the same principle. Come out strong, really get them going, convince the audience you're in control, let them relax to, "Oh, they're funny" and do your stuff. And then at the end go, "That was me. Bup bup bup bup bup". Give a big ending and have them go, "Wow. Just great" and believe it or not you will have a great show every time.

8

No Inside Jokes

What I mean by No inside jokes is that a lot of times when you're starting out you work with other comics, and you're doing coffee houses and you see the same people over and over. Well that's no excuse to be lazy. But I see it all the time. You think, "Oh, you know what, these people have seen my act. I didn't write anything today. I'm just going to do inside jokes. I'm going to talk about a bit that only my friend knows or I'm going to play to the back of the room," which is basically just trying to make other comics laugh. It's not professional, and you're not going to get anywhere doing inside jokes. To me, again, that goes back to wasting time. If you're going to do inside jokes, do it off the stage. If you want to talk about someone who's another comic, don't do it on the stage. Stage time is for professionals. Stage time is to work through material that can make a regular audience laugh. If you're doing inside jokes and only making comics laugh, that's not good because they're not your audience.

9

Audience Laughter

When you're performing, you're going to notice how the audience laughter builds. Audience laughter builds from front to back. That's always the way it is. That's why when you seat people at a comedy show, always seat them close to the stage. You want the people close and then if you have to, fill in the back. You don't want to have the back and have nobody up front. Why? Because the closer they are, the better the show is.

The reason is proximity. If people are up close, they feel that there's more of a connection. You're able to look them in the eye. There are no more distractions. If I'm in the front row and I'm looking at a comic, I'm not distracted by anything. They are there in front of me.

If I'm in the back, well the bar's in the back. There are people talking at other tables that I can listen to. There are people in front of me so I'm going, "Oh, look at that. Oh, look at that." There are a lot of

239

distractions, so you really want people all in the front and those are your anchor people. If you can get the people in the front to laugh, it builds.

What you want to do is make sure you focus on those first couple of rows up front and then let the audience build towards the back of the room. I guarantee you if the people in front aren't laughing, you're not having a good show. It will never be, "Oh the people in back think you're great but the people in front think you stink." That's not the case. You always have to get the people up front on your side because you're closest to them not only in proximity, but just in a connective way. So get them on your side and as they laugh, it will build towards the back. That's why again when booking rooms, you want to fill in the front rows first and then go towards the back.

Watch the Tonight Show now with Jay Leno as opposed to maybe tapes from when he first started. He actually moved the set. Why did he move the set? So he could have the people closer. He felt as though when he first did the monologues, they were too far away and he was right. Now he comes out, he can high five people.

Comedy Career Management by **Barry Neal**

He's doing the act and he's much closer. You want to be as close — you want to be able to almost touch the audience. When you're close to them, there's that connectiveness. That's why the worst thing in the world is when we'll talk about layout of a room in a little bit, but if you're there and there's a moat between you and the audience, you lose that relationship. You lose that connectiveness. That's why Jay moved his set and again, I don't think it's any coincidence that he moved the set and he's now the king of late night.

10

Commit To The Joke

The last thing I want to mention about performance is the commitment. You must commit to the joke. You have to believe in your joke. If you don't believe in it, why on earth would the audience believe in it? So when I say commit, commit mind, body and soul. You believe in that joke. You wrote that joke. Commit to it. Give your energy. Give your focus. Give your belief. People sense it if you believe in something.

Have you ever noticed when someone tells you something and you kind of sense they're lying because they're not saying it with much conviction? They're kind of looking around. There's no commitment to it because they're not exactly telling you the truth. If you're telling a joke, believe in the joke. Commit to it. Look people in the eye. Don't back down from the joke. I believe in this.

So again, if you commit to it, they'll at least commit to your commitment and they'll at least listen and give you a fair shake. And that's pretty much what you need to do with performance.

11

Handling the Microphone

Now I'd like to talk about surroundings. The first thing you have to deal with as a comic is the microphone. You really have to start learning how to use it, because it becomes an extension of your hand.

There are a lot of things that can go wrong with using a microphone. If you're talking and the microphone is tuned too low, the microphone's not picking you up. Conversely, a lot of people talk softly, and all of a sudden you're just booming and there's echoes and it's just a terrible sound.

Learn how far you have to be from the microphone. Different voices have to be different distances away. You have to do what's called a sound check. Before the show, go to the club and say, "Check one two. Check one two. Is this better? Is this better?" Find out where the microphone is comfortable for you for your voice.

The other decision you should make about the microphone is if you want to carry it around. Sometimes people want it just in a stand. Some people just talk and they use their hands. That's fine. If you want to keep it in the stand and you want to do your jokes and you've got your hands free, that's fine.

If you're going to take it out of the stand, I know this is going to sound stupid -- learn how to take it out of the stand. What? How difficult can it be? Well, it can be, because sometimes it's wrapped around and I've seen people take the microphone out and go, "Okay. Um." And they're doing this motion trying to unwrap it and "Uh. Hold on a second folks." And they finally get it free from the stand, and then they take the stand out of the way.

If it takes you that long, the audience is immediately going to assume you don't know what you're doing. You have to smoothly transition. When you see the microphone in the stand and it's wrapped around the stand, you have to say, "Well, thank you very much. It's nice to be here," and start doing your first joke as you're unwrapping it around. You take the stand. Get it out of the way.

Take the stand and get it out of the way. Don't just take the mike out of the stand and start talking, because if I had a stand in front of me, all you're going to be thinking as the audience is, "Hey, why is that microphone stand still in front of him?" and you're just going to sit there like that. Little things like that are going to change the image of your show, so learn how to handle the microphone. Learn how to get up on stage, grab the microphone, take it out of the stand, unwrap it from the stand if it's wrapped around it, and move the stand out of the way.

<u>Very important</u>. If you have a microphone stand and you're going to walk around, stand out of the way. Now I have a different microphone now and the reason I got this one is because some microphones like I said, they tangle a little bit, but you don't want to just grab it out of the mic stand. Because sometimes you grab it out of the mic stand and you go, "Well, thank you very much" and oops, and I've seen it happen I'd say at least 30 times in my career. It's happened to me, and all of a sudden you're like, "Uh. Well. Folks, uh, be with you in a second." It's a real easy thing. Three knobs. Three knobs. You just pop it right in, but believe me when it pops off on

stage and you're nervous, it can sit there and look like forever. "Um. Hold on, folks. I'll get it in a second. And boy, if I had a dollar for every time I've said that to a girl. Uh. Okay. There you go." If that happens to you, you've almost lost the entire audience because you don't know how to handle the microphone. The audience is going to think if you can't take a microphone out of a stand, and you don't know how to put a microphone together, how good can you be? How professional can you be?

You have to get used to handling the microphone, having the distance, how far it is, and just walking around with it, making sure that this stays here, making sure you don't hold it in the wrong place, because that's going to cause a crackled sound.

You have to get comfortable with your surroundings and realize that the one most important thing there is something that you absolutely must know how to handle. You cannot have a comedy show without a microphone. It makes all the difference in the world. Know how to handle one of these because once you do, at least you're half way home.

12

The Stage

So what else should you know about the surroundings? You have to know about the stage that you're going to be standing on. Different stages have different looks. Now a lot of times you're going to look at the background and just — you'll be able to make fun of the stage, or maybe you'll have a goofy mural and you'll be able to say something funny about that. It might have a theme, like a Hawaiian theme and just go, "Wow, I feel like I'm back in Gilligan's Island."

If you know the stage, one, you can kind of make fun of it a little bit. You can have fun in terms of the décor. Also, you'll know if the stage is set in a certain way where maybe you can't stand too close to the audience because maybe if you're at the very front of the stage, the audience is almost looking up your nose and you can't have that. Or, if you're too far back in the stage, now I'm too far from the front row, so you've got to feel for the stage. It's almost like home court advantage, the more you're on it, the more comfortable you'll be. You don't have to look down and say, "Okay, where are the dead spots?" I know where I need to be on the stage.

In addition to getting familiar with the stage, it's important to be aware of the lighting setup and the layout of the room. We're going to get to that shortly. Again, think of a stage in terms of 'this is your home'. A blind person can walk around their home because they've been there enough, so get up on that stage as much as you can before the show, before people walk in, so you're comfortable knowing that you can walk five paces this way, five paces that way and still be in everyone's sightline. Get comfortable with the stage. That's your home.

13

Lighting

The important thing about being onstage is making sure you are well lit at all times. On certain stages, if you go too far to your left or too far to your right, you're no longer lit. If you are not in the light, you are not funny. Period. People are going to wonder, "How come this person doesn't know they're in the light?" That's just what they think and the reason it's difficult is because sometimes you don't know if you're in the light. Now granted, if you have a spotlight on you, you'll know. It's in your eyes. You can't see anything. But a lot of times the room is lit a certain way. You don't know how well you're lit in a certain way.

The answer? Just another reason to get there early to see the lights and maybe have your buddy, have the other act say, "Hey, you know what, you go too far, you're out of the light" and look down and say,

"Okay, this is the marker." Maybe put a piece of tape and just go, "Don't go past this point. Don't go past this point. Don't go too close or you're too hot, you're too well lit." Know your lighting situation. You have to be well lit because you have to be seen. People have to see your eyes and your face, and maybe your arms, or whatever. They need to see you. Stand-up Comedy is also a visual art form, with every facial expression you use being a tool.

Make sure you're well lit because again, if you're out of the light, you're out of luck.

14

<u>Club Layout</u>

Another reason you want to get on the stage before the show starts is to check the layout of the room. Get up on the stage, look around and say, "Okay, where is the majority of the audience going to be sitting?" If they'll be sitting right in front of me, great. I can do my act. I can say things over here and play a little bit to this side and play a little bit to that side. Some rooms unfortunately are *weighted,* which means most of the people are on this side and a few are on this side. You want to always play to the majority. That makes sense, so I'll do most of my act this way and occasionally I'll do my act this way.

Sometimes a room is poorly seated, with the people not facing directly toward the stage, so I can't do my act all the way to these people because now these people are just getting my butt and you can't have that, so you really try to just play dead on. You play straight on and you maybe play an angle so those people can see you, and you play an angle the other way so the rest of the people can see you.

Again, play to the majority of people in the room. Have you ever noticed how much some comedians pace back and forth while doing a comedy concert on a big stage? They're trying to play to the entire, wide front rows, across the whole stage.

That's why it's so important for you to see the layout of the room and make sure people never see your backside. Watch a late night television show and notice that there is always a short musical interlude while the host walks from his monologue spot to his desk. This is because if they see your backside, you're literally turning your back on them, and they'll turn their back on you.

15

Troublemakers

I know we talked about hecklers in the previous sections, but again, with your surroundings one of the things that you want to watch out for is troublemakers. I like to watch the people even as they come in to the room. You can usually tell who the troublemakers are going to be. Sometimes they're in a large group. Quite often they're already drunk. They've may even have some noisemakers. They're looking for trouble.

A lot of times people will come up to me before the show and say, "Hey, can you make fun of my friends? They're really looking for trouble tonight. "Hey make fun of my boyfriend. He loves it when people make fun of him." I never make fun of those people because if you want to get made fun of, you're only looking for attention. You're looking to be a heckler. Those are the troublemakers. Watch. Watch where they're seated because the important thing is if you know roughly where they're seated, you'll be able to handle it.

People in the audience don't realize that when you're onstage, you usually can't see past the first or second row. Sometimes you won't even see that if it's a bright spotlight, and usually that's not good, especially if you want to look at people way in the back.

If I know where the troublemakers are seated, I'll say, "Ah. I see. They're stage left about 10 rows back." If they start heckling, I can look in that general vicinity, and go, "Hey, I know where you're seated. Believe me, I can still kick you out" or whatever the line may be. Know where the troublemakers are. Know what the layout of the room is, and you'll be able to stop any potential problems.

16

<u>The Bill Drop</u>

After you've been doing comedy long enough, you'll experience what's called a *bill drop*. That's when, towards the end of the evening, the waitress or waiter is going to drop a bill on the table. What will now happen is you'll lose control of the room, and there's just no way to avoid it, because quite frankly, everyone's having a good time and all of a sudden a bill comes and they're going to go, "$70? This show isn't as good as I thought." Or what they'll probably do is they'll go, "Oh. Who had those extra four Heinekens? Hey, did you have the nachos? I need another $7 from you. Honey, did you bring any money?" People will be talking amongst themselves because they have to figure out how to contribute for the tab.

Hopefully, if they do it well, one of two things will happen. One, they drop the bill after the show is over. I always prefer that. Or two, they kind of scatter the bill drops by not giving them to all the tables at once - because if that happens, I lose everybody. So if they scatter it, I just let the people who are talking talk, and I move to the people who aren't talking. And then when the remaining tables get their bill drop, I go back to the other people. It's best to know in advance when and how the bills will be delivered to the tables. It's a very difficult process, and one that you will only experience when you're headlining, because they never bring bills during the first half of the show, when the feature act is on.

Sooner or later, every evening, it will happen. The bill drop comes, and for the next 10 minutes you aren't going to have the complete attention of the audience. During that brief period, I try to do material that's what I call *fluff*. This material doesn't require the audience to concentrate too hard on, so it's not imperative that they're really listening. It's not something that I have to set up for a call back. It's just kind of fluff material that if you're listening to, you'll laugh. You'll have a good time, but it's stuff that I just want to get out of the way so those 10 minutes can pass while they pony up their money, and then I can finish up my last 10 or 15 minutes and close on a strong note.

So don't be alarmed. When the bill drop comes, audience attention will drop down, but it will pick back up once all the money's collected and they're set to listen again.

17

The Drink Drop

There are times when you're going to be performing and the focus will shift - and it can shift for a lot of reasons. Maybe a drink drops and all of a sudden there's the sound of breaking glass. Well that happens. And when that happens, people are going to look over and say, "What just happened? What drink dropped?" So whatever joke you're in, lose it. That joke is over. You can't go back and go, "Hey remember I was talking about the joke about the pixie sticks?" Forget it. Move on. Do the next joke.

Focus might shift for a lot of reasons. Maybe someone sneezes loud and everyone laughs. Or a cell phone will start to ring. If something like that happens, you have to give attention to that. You can't just ignore it. If no one heard the person sneeze other than you and a few people, fine. But if the cell phone goes off in the middle of the joke, in the middle of the room, you can't ignore it. More often than not, most comics will take that cell phone from the person. One of the jokes that everyone seems to do now is that they take the cell phone when it's ringing and they'll go, "Wazzup" and it gets a huge laugh. And then they'll banter with the person on the phone.

To ignore it is ridiculous. You are not being in the reality of the situation and the audience is going to go, "What's going on? Everyone knows the cell phone is going off. Do something." Don't just pretend it's not happening.

Now for me, when a drink drops, I like to approach it from a semi-serious tone, which is, "Hey, is everyone okay?" because I don't like to be just a jerk and go, "Hey, don't you dare be dropping drinks on my shift." So first, I just ask, "Is everyone okay" and then if I hear giggling and everyone's okay, then I'll make light of it and I'll say, "You know if you could have dropped that a few seconds later, it would have really wrecked the punch line. Good job!" And then I just move on. So just acknowledge the focus shift and move on.

18

<u>Listen To Them</u>

You really want to listen to the audience when you are performing. They are part of your surroundings just as much as the lights and the microphone. You have to pay attention to the audience. They are a living and breathing thing. They are the people you are having a relationship with. If you do not listen to them, they will soon not be listening to you.

Now again, they may not verbally be telling you things, but their body gestures, their energy, you can sense it. If you're having a conversation with someone and they start to yawn, what's that telling you? They're looking at their watch. What's that telling you? Listen. Get them involved. Do something. Snap them out of their trance. Do whatever you have to do, but make sure they're listening, because you have to be listening to them. Be in tune with what they're telling you. If they're telling you they're bored, switch it up. Do something else. Because if you stop listening to the audience, they will stop listening to you.

19

Denis Leary

One of my favorite comics is Denis Leary. He's from Boston. He's on the cable TV show *Rescue Me* right now and he once was on a show called "Sit Down, Stand up" with Alan King, where he made a great analogy. He said, "Stand-up is like boxing." And I was listening thinking, "Well, what does that mean?" And he was right. You kind of come out and you spar a little bit because you have to feel out the audience. You can't wildly just swing like a maniac because you don't know them and they don't know you. They have to get comfortable, so you spar. You prove, "Hey I'm funny. Bang. I'm funny. Bang. I'm funny. Bang." And when they let their defense mechanisms down and they relax and they know you're funny, boom, you hit them with a big shot.

So it's a dance. You spar with them and then you hit them. You set them up, and then boom - punch. And that's the relationship between the audience and a comic, so it is a little bit like boxing. You do that boxing dance. It's a science.

So again, listen to the audience. Set them up. It's so great when there's that pause because what that pause means is they're listening and they're ready for it. Bang, you hit them with it. Young comics all the time are scared of the silence. I know I was, so we would talk yada, yada, yada, yada. We're talking too much and we weren't letting the audience ever relax.

By boxing with them and setting them up, what you realize is that silence is perfect, because that silence just before the punch line means they're ready, there's an anticipation, then, Boom! You hit them. And wow, the waves of laughter come and then you do it all over again. Set up. Set up. Laugh laugh laugh. You wait. They're paused. It's silent. Bang! That's when you hit them again. And that's the art of it. So it's a little bit like boxing.

20

<u>**Break Down Those Walls**</u>

I've mentioned earlier that stand-up comedy is a relationship between the performer and the audience. What we want to do when dealing with the audience and the surroundings is break down those walls. Remember how we discussed the masks and revealing them? Well again, when you break down those walls, that's when the relationship can blossom.

We covered hurting your friend by pushing the right buttons because you know a lot about them? That's what you need to do. You need to break down those walls. Use all your surroundings. Use the microphone, the lights. You have all the power to get them to believe in you and trust you. Let them in on your world. You break down your walls. You listen to them. People love it when you listen.

Believe me, talk to any girl. Go out on a date and they will love it when you are listening to them. Every guy can talk about himself at length. And even though stand-ups are up there talking, what audiences love is when you're listening to them. You let them laugh. You let them feel as though they have a little control over how the mood is going, how the energy is flowing.

Believe me, we play off each other. When the audience's energy is flowing, mine is flowing. It goes back and forth and again, it's a rhythmic thing. It's sexual in a way. And the audience loves that. There's a high that's happening there.

So break down those walls of the relationship. Just say, "Listen, I'm going to be real. I'm going to reveal who I am. I want you to let your walls down, let your defense mechanisms down so we can have this great intimate moment for 40 minutes or 10 minutes." So break down those walls, because once they're broken down, the relationship can flourish. It's beautiful. It's magic.

21

Good Timing

People ask, "What is good timing? Why do Jerry Seinfeld and all the good comics have such good timing?" Good timing is also good listening. Remember how we discussed listening to an audience? That's all timing is. That's why people want comedians as actors, as commercial actors, because you need perfect timing. Michael J. Fox is probably the king. I don't think he did stand-up, but boy did he have perfect timing. You need to just wait just that beat and then hit them.

Comedy can be thrown off by merely a fraction of second. It is amazing to me that when I miss a joke, I realize afterwards or I watch the tape and I go, "Oops, I did it just too fast. I didn't wait long enough." Or "I waited just a little too long. I lost my timing." Good timing means being a good listener. That's all it is. If you can listen to the audience, you'll know when to hit them with the joke. And again, that comes with experience. So don't just be up there doing a monologue and not listening. Have a dialogue. The audience is part of what you're doing. Without them, you're just a crazy person talking. So again, good timing means good listening.

And the last thing that we're going to say in this Section is again, how many shows before you judge yourself? One hundred shows. I've said it before; I'm going to say it at least one more time. One hundred shows. Don't get down. It's so easy to lose track of where you're at when you've only done 70 shows and you're thinking, "I'm not doing well." Don't worry. Don't even think about it. Don't even look at it. Wait 100 shows, then start saying, "Okay, I have to get tougher on myself." Keep working. Have a plan. If you fail the plan, you plan to fail. Give yourself hard work. Go up there with a purpose. One hundred shows.

SECTION V:
BOOK ROOMS, SHOWCASING
And GETTING PAID

1

Finding a Room

Now that you've finally got your solid 15 minutes, you probably want to go out on the road, because you think you're good enough to open a show. But in order to go out on the road, you have to find the rooms... and where do you find them?

I could list all of the clubs here in this book, but they open and close, so the best thing to do is go to <u>comedy.com</u> and use their "Find A Club in Your City" feature. Go to comedy websites. You will see different clubs that will open up. The other way to do it is just to network. Go to your local comedy club and start asking comics. Most comics know all the clubs, certainly in their area, and most of them know other clubs in the surrounding towns. The best thing to do, go to your clubs in your area, start talking to comics. Be nice. Be open. Be friendly. Most comics know every club in their town. By surfing and networking with comics, it shouldn't take you more than a few days or a week to find out about 50 different clubs that you can contact to book a room.

2

<u>Get Out Of Town</u>

If you're reading this book and you live in Los Angeles or New York City, here's the best piece of advice I can give you. Move away. I know that sounds like I'm being flippant, but I'm serious. The problem is that Los Angeles and New York are the two main hubs of comedy. This means that if you live there, it's really difficult to get stage time because the best comedians in the country are in those towns, and you just can't compete with them for stage time.

There are only a few clubs in Los Angeles where comics can actually go and perform in front of really good crowds -- The Improv, The Laugh Factory, The Comedy Store, The Icehouse. There are a few others here and there, but as far as full-time clubs, that's about it. How many comics are there in L.A.? Thousands - so the problem is we can't give stage time to everyone, so only the best of the best work. This means that if you're in L.A. and just starting out, you're always going to be relegated to doing coffee houses, mostly in front of other comics. It is really difficult to get good when you're only performing at coffee houses or performing for other comedians. You really need to get out on the road to work.

The best way to get out there is maybe move to a different city. If you were to live in the mid-west, and I'll just pick a city. I'll pick Chicago. It's my hometown. If you live in Chicago, you are within six hours of probably forty full-time comedy clubs. Well, just imagine how much work you can get. You only have to drive five or six hours, and you've go 40 clubs.

You know how many workable clubs you're close to in L.A.? I can only think of one. There are a couple in Las Vegas, but you're not going to be working Vegas if you're starting out. You'd have to drive up to Sacramento. There are some clubs there, but they mostly use San Francisco comics.

Get away from the coasts. You're much more likely to get work if you live in the mid-west. And there's great comedy out there. You go to Minnesota, there are great comics and great clubs. The same with Michigan and in the city of Indianapolis,.

If you're in L.A., it's an invitation-only town. If you're not invited, you're not part of the party. So if you're not one of the people who are consistently getting spots at the top clubs, you're going to be working in coffee houses for a long, long time and it'll be really difficult to get better at your craft.

The same principles apply in New York. The best of the best are in New York. So again, get away from the coasts. I'd rather be a big fish in a small pond than get lost in the big pond here in L.A. And believe me, if you're good, even if you live in a small town, people around the country will know who you are.

The agents sometimes will go out to your town, certainly for the festivals, the big festivals, the Montreal festivals, the Aspen festivals. They go to places like Houston, Indianapolis, Detroit. They go to these towns to find the best comics, and then they invite them to L.A. and that's how you want to get known. You want to be invited out here. You don't want to just run out, try to bang on the door and get into the party because, that's not how it works. So go out, if you can, move to a smaller city. Become the best or one of the best in that city and eventually people will find out who you are, including the L.A. people, and you will be invited out. And it's so much better to have that ticket, that invitation that says, "You're welcome to our party."

3

<u>Burning Bridges</u>

Let's say that now you've found a couple clubs you're working at. Don't burn bridges until you're ready. Here's my point. A lot of times you're going to move up the comedy ladder and you're going to say, "I don't want to work for that person because he books lousy rooms."

Okay, maybe he does. Maybe the person that you're talking to books what we call "one-nighters" in bars, and they're not the best clubs in the country. However, be really careful. It's a small community. You burn a bridge, you're never working for that person again and you never know, although they're only booking one-nighters now, they may be booking a full-time room in a year or two.

A guy I know was working at a club here in L.A., and at the time it was a small club. It maybe had 30 people on the weekends and the weekdays maybe 10 or 12 people were there. At the open mike nights, the audience was mostly just other

272

comics. After a few months, this guy became a regular at the club and he got weekday spots, and every once in a while a weekend spot. But it was kind of a hole-in-the-wall club.

To make a long story short, he went on the road and started being a feature act, and built up a pretty big ego. He came back to the club in Los Angeles and he wanted to work stuff out on a given night because he had a 'Star Search' audition the next day. He said to the club owner, he said, "Hey, I want to get up on stage and do three minutes if that's okay." Well the club owner said, "Sure. You can go on after the other people." This young comic said, "Well I just need three minutes. I'm a regular. I shouldn't have to wait for all the open mike guys to finish. I want to go and go when at least there are people in the audience." The club owner said, "No." The young comic who had an ego said, "Yeah, I really think I should. I've worked long enough. I've worked at your door taking money. I've put in my time, so just give me the three minutes." The club owner refused, told him if he didn't like it, to hit the road.

The young comic told him to "F off". Well, as luck would have it for this young comic, this club became really one of the most prestigious clubs in the country. Investors put a lot of money into the club. The club is really one of the top clubs in the country. The young comic went back years later under a stage name because he had joined the Screen Actor's Guild. He also had a little bit of a different look, and through a referral, got three stage spots that week on, Thursday, Friday and Saturday.

The young comic went up onstage Thursday in front of a crowd of probably 200 people, just killed, had a great set. And he went up to the club owner, and the club owner said, "Ah, really good. Do I know you?" And the young comic made a really fatal mistake. Instead of denying it, he said, "Hmm, maybe. I think we might have met a few years ago. I'm not sure." The club owner nodded and he said, "How many more spots do you have this week?" and the young comic said, "I've got two. I've got one Friday and one Saturday." The club owner said, "Not anymore."

People remember. They have really long memories. They're like elephants. If you tell someone to F off, you burn a bridge, they will remember. Now that would be a funny story to me except that young comic is me. I regret saying that. I can still get spots at this club if I need to, if an important showcase is coming up. But I'll never be a regular there.

Be careful who you tell to take a hike. If you have to, bite your lip, walk away and tell your girlfriend, your wife, your friends, what a jerk they were. But you know what? Don't tell them to their face, because it's a bad business move. You never can tell when you may need them at some point. You might never need any one particular club, but if you tell enough people to F off, pretty soon you're going to be doing comedy in your garage, with your mother behind the video camera.

4

Unsolicited Material

At this point you may be asking "How do I actually start getting work? What do I send out? What do I do?" Well, here's the real info on that. Don't pay any attention to what a lot of people tell you (especially books and people who don't really know comedy) when they say, "Send out a demo tape. Get a resume. Get a headshot. Send it out to 50 clubs and then start calling." If you want to waste a couple of hundred bucks in postage, you can do that. But I would advise against it.

Never send anything unsolicited. Here's the problem. I only book a couple of colleges and a room one night a week. I get inundated with tapes. There's no way I can watch all of them. Now, I can only imagine someone who books one, two, three full-time clubs. You have to deal with openers, features, headliners, and if you are booking the room and you own the room, well now you also have to worry about the staff, the rent, all these other things. You don't have time to look at tapes, especially tapes from people you don't know. So to send anything unsolicited, you might as well just send them a copy of *Baywatch*, because they'll probably watch that more than they'll watch your tape.

Here's what you need to do. You need to find out 1) who is in charge of the room? Is it the owner or is there a booker? Find out who it is. 2) Keep calling until you get them on the line. If they don't know who you are, you're actually more likely to get them on the line at least once. When you get them on the line, do what you need to do. Lie. Cheat. Steal. Do not let them off the line because once they hang up, you may never get them on the line again.

Bookers are very, very difficult people to get hold of. And you're going to get this a lot, "Oh. So and so's not in. Can they call you right back?" If you're new, you'll say, "Sure. Here's my number..." And they'll never call. Ever. When I was starting in the business, I left my number thousands of times. I don't think I've gotten a call back more than five or six. It's just a line they use to get you off the phone. So keep calling until you get them on the line.

And again, once you have them on the line, you're like a car dealer. You ever go to a car dealership? They will not let you walk out that door if they think that they are close to a deal. Why? Because they know once you walk out that door, you're not coming back. The sale is effectively over.

It's the same principle on the phone, so do what you need to do when you're on the phone to get them to book you. And if they won't book you, at least keep them on the phone long enough to convince them to say, "Hey, I'm sending a demo tape (or DVD) out. Here's what I do. Look for it in about a week," and when after he gets it, keep making follow-up calls.

We're going to give you some phone tips in a little bit, but I really wanted to stress that one point. Don't send things out unsolicited. If they don't know it's coming, don't send it. You should also know what things you can do while you're on the phone to convince the people, "Book me right away." It's in the next chapter.

5

The Assistant's Name

All right, let's say you've called the club. The booker will almost never answer his or her own phone. Sometimes they have their own line, but more often than not, you have to call the club and ask for the person in charge, whether it's the owner who books it or the booker themselves.

Assuming you're not going to get the booker on the line, There's going to be a girl or a guy answering the phone. They are the guardians. They are the gatekeepers to keep you, the comic, away from the booker. What do you do? The best thing you can do is learn their name. It's really important. They're young kids usually, 18 to 22, answering the phone. Don't just say, "Hi, I'm looking for Bill" because they'll go, "Who is this?" "This is Barry Neal." "Hold on." "He's not in right now. Can he call you right back?" I guarantee you, he's there. He just not in to Barry Neal. If I said Jerry Seinfeld, he'd absolutely be in. I always find it funny when they say, "Hold on a second" and it's like I know they're going to ask, "Hey, do you want to talk to Barry Neal?"

Here's what you want to do. You want to make friends with the person who is the gatekeeper. So what I'll say, "Oh, who is this? Julie?" I'll write down her name. "Great, listen, I'll call back in a day or two. Here's my number. Thanks so much." And I call back in a day or two. Pretty much it's always the same person. I go, "Hey, Julie. How are you doing?" And after five or six times of doing this, they get to know who Barry Neal is.

Empower that. Make them feel good because after five or six calls and I haven't gotten through, I'll say, "Julie, listen. I don't want to waste your time. I love talking with you. What do you think is a good idea? When is a good time to call?" Well now it empowers that person on the phone. Quite frankly, they're just a phone person, but it makes them feel good and they may give you some inside tips saying, "You know what? He gets in from lunch around 1 o'clock. So one to two, he's always in and I'll make sure he takes the call." Or if nothing else, "He's in from one to two and I'll see what I can do."

Make them feel good. If you can get the gatekeeper on your side, it's at least one way to get to the booker.

6

Phone Tricks

There are certain tricks you can use to make somebody book you. I hate calling them tricks, but that's really what they are. The booker, if they don't know who you are, will tell you, "Oh, send a videotape." Again, that's just a nice way of telling you "good night and good luck." You'll send the tape. You'll call again and again and again... all to no avail.

Most comics will tell you tapes don't work. I can't think of more than three or four jobs at clubs I've ever worked in my career that I got off a tape. One, you're not funny in tapes. Two, there are too many tapes that bookers have to look at. They just can't look at enough tapes. So how are you going to get them to book you? You have to figure out your own tricks. I'll tell you some of mine.

When I started out, I would tell them, "Oh, I'm in town." I just happen to be in Des Moines that week. I'd give them enough leeway and I'd call up and I'd say, "You know, I'm in town in June." I'm in town for a wedding, a bar mitzvah, an anniversary, who cares what it was, but I'm in your town. Hey, how fortunate for you. You don't have to pay for my airfare. You don't have to pay me anything extra. I'm from L.A. I happen to be a headliner. But you know what, I'm in town and I'm willing to feature. Knock yourself down a rung so when they feel like they're getting you, they're getting a bargain.

When I wanted to feature, I would always say I'm a headliner. You know why? Because as a booker, when somebody tells me they're headliner and I've never heard of them, I assume they're a feature. I've never met a feature that didn't think they were a headliner. It's like every U.S. Senator, who sees a President whenever he looks into a mirror. When someone says they're a feature, it usually means they're an opener. They're a good opener maybe. But they're not really a feature consistently. And if someone tells me they're an opening act, it means they're just hungry for work and are probably doing a lot of open mikes. That's just the nature of the beast. I wish I could tell you it was different, but it's not.

People exaggerate their abilities, so a headliner to me is really a feature. A feature is really an opener, and an opener is really an M.C. But what if I really am a headliner? Well, then you're probably so arrogant, you're thinking, "I usually don't play comedy clubs, but I'm in town." Most bookers know every headliner. If you're a headliner and a good one, your name has been out there long enough where you don't have to sit there and tell people you're a headliner. We know who you are.

So again, let the bookers feel good about themselves. "Hey, I headline a lot of rooms. Blah blah blah. But I'm going to be in Des Moines for a wedding. Why don't you let me work the week?" Give them enough lead time though. Don't tell them you're doing it next week. Most headliners are booked six to twelve months in advance. Most feature acts are booked four to six months in advance. Most openers are booked three to four months in advance, so you've got to give the booker that lead time. If it's January and you want to work in June as a feature, say, "I'm going to be out in June for a wedding. Hey, why don't we just work then?" What they may say is this, "Hey, that sounds great. I'll put you down in pencil." <u>Then</u> send a videotape. That's why you need a demo tape or DVD. It's not getting you the work, but it won't prevent you from getting the work. Send it out. They may look at it. They may not look at it. But at least send it out and then call back in a month and just say, "Hey, I'm putting it down in pen that we're all ready for June" and unless your videotape is awful, you'll get the work.

Here's a trick I did and I'm not saying you should do it, but it worked for me. There were two clubs in Denver at the time. One was downtown and one was on the north end. And these two guys were friends, so what they would do is they would book a headliner one week here in the north club and then one downtown the following week. I tried for years, like two and a half years, to get into these clubs but couldn't get anywhere. I phoned them. I sent tapes I phoned again. Nothing. Finally, I thought to myself, "Okay, I gotta figure out a way, because these are good clubs and I really want to work them."

So I thought about it and called up the guy in the downtown club. His name was Tim. I said, "Tim, hi, this is Barry Neal." He says, "Hi." I said, "Listen, John over at the other club already gave me a week, July 12th through the 16th. He told me to call you to get the week after from the 20th to the 24th." Did I really have that week? No. I hadn't even spoken to John. I just told Tim that I had the week headlining. And he said, "Oh. All right. Well, if John booked you, I'll put you in pencil. Send me a videotape and I'll talk to John." I said, "Great." Jotted those dates down for the 20th through the 24th, and I hung up and I quickly called John. I said, "John, hi, this is Barry Neal. Tim down at the downtown club headlined me from the 20th to the 24th and he said I should call you and get the week before, the 16th to the 20th." And he said, "Oh, well, if Tim already booked you, all right I'll pencil you in. I'll talk to Tim. Send me a tape."

I never sent a videotape to Tim. I never sent a videotape to John. I just said, 'Forget it.' I will just assume I have the work. I penciled it in and will just act as if they've spoken to each other and we're all set. A few weeks went by, so I called John. I said, "Hey, I sent my tape out and I assume you talked to Tim because I spoke to Tim and he said that he spoke to you." I don't even know if they spoke to each other, but if you think you're so important that as soon as they hang up they call each other to talk about you, you're wrong They don't do that. They just assume. Tim booked you. I'll book you. And I'm a booker, I've done that. If I get a reference from another booker, "Hey, book this guy", I just do it. I just assume the guy's not going to screw me.

I ended up working both of those weeks and I killed them both weeks and I've worked for both those clubs for years. As a matter of fact, I still work at one of those clubs. The other club went under a few years ago.

Here's a great end to the story. I'm working at the club. It was on the north side, and I see a stack of videotapes in his office. I said, "Wow, look at those tapes. do you ever look at those?" And he said, "No, people send them all the time. You know what? I'm at the club eight hours, five days a week when I go home, I am not watching more comedy." And I said, "Wow, that's really incredible. How do you get people?" He said, "referrals I have enough people." And I said, "Yeah, I thought so. I didn't think you could watch all the tapes." And he looked at me and he kind of saw the glint in my eye and he said, "You know, it's interesting. You've been working here how many years? Four or five?" I said, "Yeah."

And he said, "I don't remember ever seeing your videotape." I told him "That's because I never sent it." We both had a good laugh.

My point is this. Find out a way that you can sneak in the back door. There is no definitive way of getting work. Yes, you need a videotape. Yes, you should send it. But again, maneuver yourself on the phone. Sell yourself. Be a good salesman. Get phone technique. If you want to, I know other people that have done this. They have their wife call, act as a manager. Makes it seem more authoritative.

Act as your own manager. Get a cell phone and have the outgoing message say "This is Barry Neal Management". Of course, you should use another name. Let's say that your name is Tim, Tim Smith. Make up a name for your cell phone. "This is Scott Levinson Management." Who cares? Whenever you use this cell phone, you're Scott Levinson, and you represent a lot of clients, and you think Tim Smith should be in your room. It makes the person feel good as a booker that they know that you have a manager that's booking you. This is a part of show business. It's all make believe.

I don't know what your tricks are going to be. These are just some of the ones have worked for me. You've got to learn your own. All I'm saying is you can't always play by the rules because you won't always get in.

7

<u>Persistence</u>

Get used to the idea of being on the phone, because you're going to be on it a lot. I am still on the phone probably a few hours a week just getting bookings down, making sure the clubs still know I'm out there, and looking forward to getting more bookings.

When you send your tape out, or even if you don't send it and you're trying to get bookings, you always have to call these people. I've actually gotten booked when I first started just by pestering people. There's a fine line between being persistent and being a pest. But you're going to have to really push that envelope.

There's a club in Chicago that I still work at. Before getting hired, I called every other day. He finally got on the line and said, "You know what? You're so damned persistent I want you to stop calling" and he gave me a week. I was the opening act, and Ten years later I was headlining for him. Over the years we've become friends.

If you only call once a week, you're not going to get called back. They're not going to pick up the phone. Most of these clubs get 50 calls a day from comics. So go in their shoes. Don't just think, "Why don't they call me back?" Listen, it's not all about you. I know we like to think that. I know we like to think we are the most important people in the world, but you are just one comic, one comic in 50 that is calling on a Monday. So call Monday. Call Wednesday. Call Friday. Don't give up until they say no, and there's no reason that they're going to say no because you have good phone skills.

I've discussed being friendly. When you finally get that booker on the phone, don't say "I've left 50 messages." Just go, "Hey, Bob, how ya' doing? Listen, I know I've called a lot. I'm just really looking forward to working your club. What date can we put together? I have my book out." If they tell you, "Oh, I don't have my book with me." You can come back with "I've got my book with me, so why don't we pencil in some date in the future, and we can finalize it after you see your book." Whatever you can do when you get them on the phone, book it. Put it in pencil. Do whatever. Say, "I'll call back Monday and we'll put it in pen, but let's put something down now so when I call you, I can call and say, 'Hey, I'm just confirming that June date.'"

If you have the internet, email is also another good way. Email them. That's real easy. They may delete it, but you know what? You can email them every other day. Just a nice little note, "Just saying hello. Looking forward to working for you in June. Let me know what you have."

A lot of people will tell you to fax. You really should have a fax machine. Almost every comic I know that's successful has one now. Fax them every other day. Just keep updating. I personally don't care for the fax that much because I feel as though it goes out, they kind of look at it, and throw away.

I like to talk to the person on the phone. Often they won't get on the phone, but I just keep trying every couple of days, I get on the phone. Talk to the person who's the assistant and say, "Hey, you know, bud can I talk to Rich? Is he there?" and eventually Rich gets on the line and I just get that voice-to-voice human connection. And he'll say, "Hey, can you fax stuff?" "Sure, I'll be happy to fax it. I'm just saying these are the dates that I'm looking for." Okay.

Stay on them. Stay on them. Stay on them. Be persistent. It's very difficult, because a lot of times they won't respond. That doesn't mean they're not listening. Just keep on them. Persistence will avail. Whether they want to admit it or not, they need a constant stream of stand-up comedy talent to fill their rooms. True, there are a lot of comics out there trying to get the work, but if you develop your telephone skills and let them know that this first contact with you on the phone is only the tip of your professionalism, it will give them a good feeling. Professionals like to do business with professionals. They're all professional bookers... let them know that you are a professional too.

8

Recommendations

If you really want to work a club, the best way to get in is by being recommended. If you can't actually go to the club, get a recommendation from someone who does work at that club. If I'm working somebody, and he tells me, "I've got a guy, Joe Y, and he's fantastic." I'll think, "Oh, all right." Well, what you should do if you're Joe Y and found out that he'd been recommended, he should get right on the phone and call me up, saying something like "Hi, I'm a good friend of so-and-so, who works for you. He told me to call you. I work this club, that club, that club." And you know what? You're probably getting booked right there. If I really trust the guy making the recommendation, he doesn't throw out too many comics to me, and he says, "Look, Joe Y is fantastic." I'm booking him. So if you find out that you've gotten a recommendation from a comic who works a club, call right away.

When I'm headlining at the club and I tell you, "Hey, listen, you're funny. Call." Don't wait for me to leave the club. While I'm working at that club say, "Hi, I'm a friend of Barry Neal's. He told me to call. I work with him a lot and he said I should call." Well, the booker will probably contact me that week and say, "Oh, you know I got a call from your buddy. Is he good?" and if I did recommend you, I'll say, "Yeah, you should book him right away."

That's what you need to do. It's word of mouth. It's referral. That's how this business works. So if someone gives you a recommendation, you gotta call right away, and if you don't get through to him, you call again the next day. Keep on. Persistence.

9

Personally Showcase

The best way to get work is to personally showcase at a club. It's great if you can get a referral from a comic. It's great if you're sending tapes and you're calling and you're really persistent. But if you really want to work, the best way to do it is to personally showcase.

When you showcase, you're working for free. But what you do is you call up a club, hopefully if you have a club, maybe two or three within two or three hours. You call them up, tell them your name, let them know you're a headliner or a feature, or whatever you think you are and say, "Can I get five minutes? Ten minutes?" It's free. Almost every club in the country will let you do that. It's free entertainment. So you go up and you go do your five minutes and you destroy. Now they know who you are, so when they think of your name, they don't think, "Oh, it's just you" without an act. They think, "Oh yeah, he was the guy that killed in my room. We're going to use that guy."

Also, when you personally showcase, make sure that the manager or the booker is in the room. There's no point in showcasing if the guy who books you isn't there. So, you're showcasing, you're killing, you're doing well. The booker's there. Right afterwards, you go up and you say, "So, would you like to book me?"

It's so much easier when it's a face-to-face thing. It's not over the phone. It's so easy to say 'no' to a salesperson on the phone. You're calling up. You get those calls all the time. "Hi, I'm calling from so-and-so." "Okay. Thanks. No." But if they're face-to-face, often you have to at least listen to them. And if they're making a good deal, you may say, "That's a pretty good deal." Same thing in comedy, it's easy to say 'no' to someone over the phone. "I don't know who you are. Oh, You're a comic. Great. I got about 50 comics calling." If you're a comic, you're in my face, and I see a great act, boy I want to book you.

Comedy Career Management by **Barry Neal**

I book people all the time when they come and do my rooms for free. They come. They do it. They destroy. I say, "I gotta use this person." Personally showcasing is the way to go. If you can, call up your local clubs. Give them a little bit of time. Give them a week or so, and say, "I'd like to come next Tuesday, Wednesday, Thursday. Can I have five minutes?"

When you showcase, you're going to get a maximum of probably ten minutes. They'll usually ask you, "What position are you normally comfortable with?" They want to know where in the show you perform: are you the opener that does 15 minutes, the feature that does 30, or the headliner that does 45? When you personally show-case, they will almost never say, "Well, we'd like you to headline." Headliners are only headliners because they've been doing it a long time and the booker's absolutely convinced you are a headliner.

You can almost always be a feature or the opener when you showcase. Here's the hitch: when they ask you what position you're comfortable in, they're going to knock you down a peg. If you say "I'm usually the feature," they're going to say, "Oh, great. Can you come in as the opener so you can move up?" Always put yourself up a notch. Just like on that resume, lie a little bit. "What position are you doing?" "Uhhh... I'm a headliner." And then say, "But this is a great club. I'll be happy to come in and feature." Believe me, you tell them you're a feature, they're going to want to bring you in as the opener.

So again, no matter what spot you want, put yourself up a notch. If you really want to go in as the opener, just say, "Well, I'm pretty much a feature, but I know you have a lot of great acts here. I'll be happy to come in as the opener." But that's on the preface of, "I'm opening once or twice, but I'm really a feature." You must put that in their mind. Even though they may not really listen to it, let them know you are a feature. You're willing to come in as an opener once or twice, so when you kill, you can move up a little easier.

If you really want the work, you're going to have to drive a little, but it's worth it. Personally showcasing, you're in their face. That's really the best way to get work.

10

Re-booking

You've just completed your first week of professional work, and you're getting paid. All right! Good for you! Way to go! Now we have to talk about re-booking. You want to go back to that room. You had a great time. What's the best way to go about getting re-booked?

First, you're going to get paid. When you get paid, you're going to get paid in a check. You sign the back of the check and you get cash. Most of the time, you should take the cash. I'm not saying checks will bounce, but it can happen. And you don't want to be stuck with a bounced check. So take the cash. There's really no reason not to. Just don't go to the casino and gamble it away.

Now you want to re-book yourself. Don't leave that building until you have a date for the next time you're coming back. It's just like having them on the phone. The car dealership -- they don't let you leave the doors. Do not leave the building until you have another date set. They may say, "Oh, you know what, call next week because we don't have our books here." Don't. Once you leave the door, the new comics are coming in.

Believe me, as much as I think I'm important to me, I mean nothing to the club. I hate saying that but it's true. My picture goes down Sunday night and it's, "Barry who? Oh, you mean the guy that has to leave the hotel? Yeah. Great. We've got a new person coming in." That's just the way it works. You're always rotating new comics at clubs. So as much as you had a good time with the club, you hung out with the staff, everyone loved you, you had great shows, it's "Barry who?" by Sunday night by twelve o'clock because I'm done. So you have to try to get yourself re-booked. Bring your booking book, whatever you have, and say, "Hey, you know what? I'm available to come back in October."

Comedy Career Management by **Barry Neal**

Rule of thumb is this: Headliners work a full-time club once a year, maybe twice but usually once a year. Feature acts can work a club two times a year, maybe three, but usually twice. Openers can work a lot more. That's the one benefit of being an opener. You can work a club as an opening act, four, five, sometimes six times a year.

So summing up, know what position, whatever position you were in, if you were the opener, just say, "Hey, can I come back in two months? I've got something open that week. If you're the feature, it's "Oh you know what? I got something four or five months down the line," and If you're the headliner just say, "Do you have anything later this year?" You know, if it' s January, maybe later in the year. If not, "Hey, let's book it for January of 2002." Done. Out of the way. Because again, once you leave that room, you're out of sight, out of mind.

11

Negotiating a Fee

Let's talk money. I know you'd like to make the most amount of money you can in stand-up comedy. I understand that. In the beginning, you're not going to. You have to understand that. It's okay. There's money to be made in stand-up. A lot of comics do very, very, very well. Some of them, you've never even heard of because they do what's called *corporate shows*. So how much money can you expect to make?

In the club circuit, where they have comics all the time, they know what the market value is. Rule of thumb is this -- Opening acts, you're not going to make much. I'm sorry. You're going to make anywhere from as low as $150 for the week to maybe $350. That's the rule of thumb. Opening acts are really almost exclusively in-town people because you almost can't travel if you're only making $250. You can't fly to another city. Now again, that's why you want to be in the mid-west because you can drive 4 hours and you can pick up $250. It's not great, but it's an experience. That's why a lot of people say, "I don't even want to go out as the M.C. I'm going to work it until I have 30, 40 minutes and be a feature act."

So how much money does a feature act make? Well, again, you're doing 30 minutes in the middle. Low end is $350. That's really low. High end is $650 for the week. It's a hand-to-mouth existence being a feature act. But again, it's a stepping stone. You're doing it because that's your plan because you want to be the headliner.

Then you move up and now you're a headliner. How much can you command? There are two types of headliners -- People the average Joe headliners. They're funny. They do a great job, but they don't bring a lot of people into the seats. There's no name recognition. So if you're not a name-recognized headliner, you're going to make anywhere from $1,000 to maybe $1500 a week. Not bad money, but again not great.

If you are starting to bring people in, you start to get a little name recognition, maybe not national exposure, but in that town people know who you are for whatever reason. Maybe you have a mailing list. That's something that I have and we're going to talk about that later. It's a mailing list that you put down on the table so if they enjoy the show, they fill it out. I keep those mailing lists and the next time I come back in town, I mail all those people. I email them saying, "Hey I'm coming back in town. Come back. Bring your friends." Because now I have more people coming to see me and I have a little bit more power to say to club owners, "I bring some people in. You should now pay me a little more money."

So if you're an above the title headliner, anything goes. Just depends on how important you are and how many people you're going to bring in. A lot of times, above the title headliners are making anywhere from $2,000. I don't even want to tell you some of the numbers I've been quoted. Not for me, but for people I've talked to, $30,000 for a weekend. It's a lot of money. If you can bring people into the seats because people know who you are, the sky's the limit.

So that's the money for club circuit. Now, where's the real money to be made for the average comic, for the comic who isn't a Jerry Seinfeld or a Damon Wayans? How much money can you really make?

You can make a lot of money if you're doing what's called *corporate work*. We talked about corporate work earlier. It has to be clean. A lot of times, air bases, Air Force bases or Navy bases, or just general corporations want Christmas shows or they want someone to host a Christmas party because they're giving out awards at a banquet. These people have no clue how much comedians make. Sometimes they're on the wrong end of it. They'll call me up and they'll say, "Oh, we saw you at the club. We'd love to have you." "Oh great. What's your budget?" "Uh, $50." "Uh. That really doesn't get me out of bed." I don't do a show for $50. Most headliners wouldn't even think of it.

So how much can you really expect to make? I don't know. Let's do a quiz real fast. "I think you're funny. I saw you at the local club. I represent a business. It's a small business but we have about fifty people and we're going to have a Christmas party. We'd love for you to do 30 minutes." How much would you charge? Go ahead, think about it. What's your answer? How much are you going to charge me to do 30 minutes? Now if you're a feature act and you're used to getting $100 per show, what are you going to tell me? You going to tell me $200? You going to tell me $100? You going to tell me $500? What are you going to tell me?

Whatever you said, you're wrong. Here's why. You just made the first mistake in negotiation. First you want to find out what their budget is. So unless you ask the question, "Well it really depends. How much are you looking to spend?" because that's the only right answer there is. Why? Because you have no idea what my budget is so if I ask you how much you're willing to work for, you don't know how much I'm willing to pay.

Here's the problem. If someone asks me how much I'm willing to work for, and I say, "I'll do it for $500." And they say, "Okay". Well, what happens when I found out the rest of the people are all getting $1,000? That's happened to me. I was working at the Icehouse. This guy comes up to me and he says, "We're doing a show. We want four comics. We'd like for you to host the show." And I said, "Great!" And he goes, "How much would you charge?" And I thought, "$500." It's an in-town gig. It's maybe an hour and a half. Yeah. $500. And he's like, "Wow, that's great. Everyone else is getting $1,000." Super. That's really nice to know. I just lost $500 because I shot my mouth off.

First point in negotiation, don't quote your price. You don't know what they're willing to spend. Let's say I had said $1,000 and he was thinking, "Oh, I was looking to pay $300." I'll work for $300 in town for an hour, hour and a half; but there's nowhere for me to go. If I said $1,000, he would just turn around and say, "Ah, we don't have that kind of budget." What am I supposed to do? Turn around and say, "Oh wait. I'll work for $300." Well now I'm a liar and a thief. Do you see how that works? If you overshoot and you say, "I want $1,000" and they're looking at – "Well we were looking at paying $200 or $300," and you would have taken it, you can't say, "Oh but I'll take $200 or $300." Find out what they want. Do whatever you have to do. Ask whatever questions you have to, to manipulate that situation.

Here's what I do. People ask all the time, "I'm having a Christmas party. I'm having a birthday party." I've done those. I've been doing weddings. I do a lot of weddings now. They say, "How much would it cost for you to come in and do a wedding?" I ask questions but quite frankly,

I don't even care what the answer is. I'm just trying to get them to say what their ballpark is. I'll say, "Well, it really depends on the day of the week. Are you doing it on a Friday or a Saturday?" and I'll say, "What are you looking to spend?" And they're say, "Well, we don't know. It's a Friday or a Saturday." I'll say, "Well, there are other factors. Are there like 200 people? 300 people?" "Oh, there's like 200 people." And again, I'll say, "What kind of ballpark are we looking at?" And usually they don't realize it but that's all I'm trying to get and they'll tell me. "Well, we're looking to spend about like $1,000 or $1,500." Boom. Now I have my number.

Once you have your number, know that the first price they quote, they're low balling you. They want to see how low they can get you for. So when he says $1,000 to $1,500, I know they have more in the kitty. Now I'm not going to say, "Well, that's insane. I want $3,000." What I do is I go one and one half times. So if they say $1,000, I say, "I really pretty much do weddings for $1,500." And then I kind of feel them out. A lot of times, they'll say, "Well, yeah, we can go up to $1,500." They may not. They may really be topped at $1,000. Maybe they'll say, "Ah, you know what. Let me get back to you. I think we can get $1,200." Then I'll say, "You know what? If it's $1,200, you got a deal."

We've just negotiated. Would I have done it for $1,000 if it's in town? In a heartbeat. You're talking about 40 minutes of work for $1,000? I'd do that in a second. I would have probably done it for $500, maybe even $300 or $400 if it's close to my house. But the key is, why undersell yourself when they're willing to pay that money?

Negotiation, that's the key. The first step in a negotiation, find out what they have. Find out what their budget is. It's the same thing with a job. You're going to go in. You want a certain amount. But if you know that they pay that level of employee $50,000, what are you going to say? "I'm really just looking for $40,000." "Okay. Super. $40,000." No, they're paying $50K, So ask for $55,000 or $60,000.

Negotiation, that's really one way. Corporate parties is really the way to go and that's why I say, if you can work clean, you can do a lot of corporate. You can make a very nice living.

12

First Impressions

First impressions are what people really remember in comedy. That's why I said in the beginning that you've got to start out strong. Remember in that last Section we said that you start strong because your first impression, that first couple of jokes is the impression that the audience will have of you.

It's the same thing when you do your set. So if you go and showcase at a club, you'd better make sure that you're ready to kill, because if you go and you stink, they're not going to give you another showcase. Even if they give you another showcase in a year, their first impression is, "Oh. Yeah. That guy's coming again." Even if you're funny, they still have those hidden feelings of, "Ohhhh... I don't know. He's funny now, but he sure was terrible that first time."

First impressions are crucial. Do not play a room until you're ready. So many of my students tell me, "I'm going to go to the Improv and showcase" and I plead with them, "Please don't." Just because you had one good show at a coffee house does not mean you're ready to play with the big boys. When you have 99 out of 100 shows go great, then showcase.

Here's my rule of thumb. If you think you're ready to showcase, give yourself six months. Tape yourself. See if you are not significantly better in six months. If you're not significantly better and you're still funny, great. Showcase. But if you see yourself in six months and you go, "Wow. I am so much better. I'm so glad I didn't showcase" which I'm sure will be the case, then say, "Hmm. Maybe I should wait another six months to see where I'm at." Now I'm not saying you want to wait forever, but keep working until you get to the point where in six months, you're not significantly funnier than you were six months earlier. Those first impressions are important. They'll always remember that.

That's why sometimes you don't want to go into a club as an M.C. We'll talk about that in a little bit. But you can get pigeonholed if you're not funny or you're just funny enough to be an M.C., you may be an M.C. for a long, long time. So when you're ready, go ahead and showcase, but please, give yourself that extra six-month window. Wait six months.

13

Don't Get Pigeonholed

When you work a room, you can be pigeon-holed into that spot that you go in, so be careful. If you go in as an opening act, often times that's always what they'll see you as. When I was started out in L.A., there was a club called Igbys. It was a great club. It was a great guy who ran it. I went in too young. I went in and I was the M.C. and I was a good M.C. and I did my job well, but the problem is they will always see you as that. So whatever they first see you as, that's kind of where they pigeonhole you.

After doing Igbys for a few years being the M.C. I'd get the occasional spot, but the people who were headlining were great. I was young and I was just starting out and I was getting good experience. But the problem is, the owner always saw me as the opener. Years later, I wasn't at the club anymore and the owner actually ran a club which was a few hours outside of L.A. I had done a lot of TV shows and was headlining,

And I thought, "Oh, it'd be fun to give him a call and go out and do his club."

I called him up, and I said, "Ah, how ya' doing? This is Barry Neal." And he said, "Ah, long time no talk." I said, "Yeah. I hear things are going great with you. I hear you have a little one-nighter out there." I said, "I would love to come play it, say hello." And he said, "Super." And he said, "Yeah, listen I have an opening spot available in a month." And I just said, "I don't open anymore. I've been headlining for years. I've done all this TV." And he was like, "Ooh, we don't have anything open to headliners. We're all booked." Now he didn't. Obviously he had stuff, but he kept thinking of Barry Neal, the young opener.

First impressions are important. We talked about first impressions, right? When you first get on stage you start strong because that's the first impression you have to make. I am strong. If you're an opener, they're always going to think of you as an opener. So be careful. Don't go in to too many rooms as an opening act because you can be pigeonholed, and an opener's a very tough position. You're going up in front of a cold room. You're probably not going to be the funniest person on the bill. You have the least experience, and you have the worst spot in front of a cold audience.

It's tough. You can get pigeonholed. What you want to do is go into a room either as the feature or the headliner if you want to move up. There are certain clubs you may say, "I'm willing to be an opener there for a long time" especially in your hometown. Your hometown will never treat you with the same respect that the other towns will treat you with. Why? Because they saw you grow up, and it's tough to see somebody grow up in comedy because you see them in the beginning and they're not that funny. And it's tough to recognize how funny they ultimately become because it's such a slow process.

If you have a child, you know what I'm talking about. You see the child every day and you don't realize daily, weekly, monthly, they keep growing. But if you're the uncle and you go back once a year and you say, "Oh my god! Look how he has grown!" As the parent, you just kind of say, "Yeah. You know, I don't even realize it." Well of course, because you see the kid every day. He'll always just be your baby.

It's the same thing in comedy. Your hometown will never give you the same respect that other towns will because they saw you grow up. That's why I always tell my students you really don't want to learn from somebody who is very prominent in the business because quite frankly, they're never going to put you on that prominent stage. To think as though you're going to be a student and go through their class and be an open miker and then like a year later say, "Hey, I'm ready to hit the big time." They're always going to say, "Oh, you're my student."

That's why they want the fresh blood, the fresh people from Milwaukee and Indianapolis to come on and say, "I'm already headlining and I'm ready." People want a prepared product. People want someone who is ready and a headliner and new. They don't want to see you grow up. Granted, you have to grow up somewhere. So again, do it in your hometown. Be an opener, but again, be very careful about getting pigeonholed.

Once you're an opener in a certain club, you're probably going to be stuck as an opener there for a few years. Maybe it's a good idea to be an opener for one or two clubs, but then work really hard, so when It's is easier to jump from being a feature, the one who does 30 minutes, up to being a to headliner. That's a much easier jump than it is from being an opener to a feature, simply because the feature is such a bad position. You're going up again into that cold room, probably with no introduction. It's a very difficult situation. You have the least amount of time to actually get the audience on your side. So it's an easier jump from being a feature to a headliner than it is from an opener to a feature. So again, be careful of being pigeonholed.

14

<u>M.C.</u>

Being an opener is also being an M.C. You are the Master of Ceremonies, so you're running the show. But be aware that it's the toughest spot. Again, we talked about that. You're going up on stage. People are still being seated. The drink orders are just coming in. You're only getting 10 or 15 minutes and you probably have the least amount of experience of everyone on the bill. It's a tough spot.

Here's what you need to do. You need to have high energy. You need to be clean, and you just need to get the audience in a frame of mind that "We're going to have fun." I hate saying it, but an M.C. is just a cheerleader.

I act as the M.C. sometimes for local shows where I'm the booker, for a club that's a good client. I don't have an ego about it. They're not supposed to laugh at

317

me. Yeah, I'll tell a story or I'll tell a joke here or there and if they laugh, great.

My main concerns are to 1) get the introductions right. That's no doubt the most important job of the M.C. Make sure that you bring the audience to a level they are ready to listen and then you introduce the next comic correctly Secondly, keep the energy up. Cheerlead. "All right! Hey, we're ready to have a good time." Good M.C.'s do that all the time. They finish their set. They say, "Thank you very much. Hey folks, you ready for the next comedian?" And if the audience sits there, umm, I always say, "Folks that's not good enough. This guy's too good for that. You ready to have a good time?" and then they cheering. Get the energy level up. You're a cheerleader. That's what an M.C. is.

Sometimes it's hard on the ego being an M.C. because the audience doesn't even think of you as a comic. So many times at the Improv, people would come up when I was M.C.'ing and they'd say, "Oh, you ought to tell that comic he was funny." What am I? His lackey? And sometimes when I was even opening on the road, they would say to the comics, they'd look and they'd say, "You were funny. You were funny." And then they'd look at me and go, "Hey, you're not bad" like I'm not even a comic.

Unfortunately as an M.C., being funny is almost secondary to getting the introductions right, making sure that you plug anything that the club has to promote whether it's t-shirts or upcoming events, and saying where the bathroom is. You're the Master of Ceremonies. It's great if you're funny. It's a bonus if you're funny. But the key is, do your job, look good, look professional. I think M.C.'s should look professional because it's kind of your show. You're welcoming the audience. But again, are you the funniest person on the bill? No. So be careful when you're pigeonholed as the opener because it's a tough rut to get out of.

15

A, B and C Rooms

There are several different types of clubs that you're going to play. We'll talk about the 'A' rooms first. An A room is a top room in the country. The way to tell that something is an A room is they usually do comedy at least four days a week, sometimes five maybe six. If they're doing it that often, they're doing something right. Those clubs are usually bringing in the best headliners, people who are making top money. And even if they're not bringing in big, big names, they're bringing in guys that are really good headliners.

So it's though if you're just starting out to think, "Well maybe I can feature that room" because if you're featuring that room, you're probably headlining most other rooms, so you're not somebody that's just beginning to feature. When I headline those rooms, those features will tell me all the time, "Normally, I headline" and they probably normally do. But the fact of the matter is, if you're just starting out, you really have to be an opener in the A rooms.

The B rooms are a little bit different. B rooms just don't do comedy quite as often. Maybe they're Friday, Saturday or Thursday, Friday, Saturday. They have to pay a little bit less. They don't have the same budget.

Headliners there are making usually closer to the $1,000 range, maybe $1,100, $900 sometimes. So the features they're not making the $650s. They're making close to the $400, $450 range. So you're more apt to be a feature act there if you're just starting out a year or two into it than being an opener. Usually, they don't even have an opener in those rooms or if they do, they're local kids. They're paying them $50 a show so they're only making $150. So those are B rooms.

Then there's something called C rooms a.k.a. hell gigs. A lot of times you're going to work in a bar, you're going to work in a restaurant. Now often they're called hell gigs, but they can be fun. The headliner's going to do it, probably make $200 a show. The feature act will do it. He'll make $100. There may or may not be an opener. Usually in C rooms, there's not even an opening act. It's a two-person show.

They're called hell gigs because they're in a bar and a lot of times it's going to be noisy. It's going to be maybe a little rowdy. They might like rather blue language. It's just a tougher room. They're not going to really go for intellectual stuff that often.

Sometimes you are going to get a one-nighter that is professionally run. I know I'm biased, but quite frankly, one club I run is a dinner theater. It's an older clientele, and we are bringing in some of the best names in the country. But that's Los Angeles.

If you're in a different town and you're doing a one-nighter, it's probably in a bar, and it's going to be rough. But you know what? You have to go through those rooms because if you can entertain those people, then it's a lot easier to go to a regular comedy club where they're used to comedy and make them laugh. So those are the 3 types of rooms: A rooms, B rooms, and C rooms.

16

Don't Poke Where You Joke

Now you're at a club. You're working for the week. Things are going great. What are you going to do? Well, I suggest bring some books. Bring video games. Do what you need to do and keep writing.

At night, you're going to want to do stuff. That's fine. You're going to want to hang out with the staff. They're the only people you know in this town, so hang out with them if you want. Go play some pool. Get a drink. Do what you have to do but please, do not screw the help.

I know you're laughing, going, "What?! Comics and waitresses." I know. Comics and waitresses go together like peanut butter and jelly. It's great. However, if you do it, you're really begging for trouble. You know, you don't poop where you eat. You don't screw where you work. It's just a bad idea.

Here's why. You end up hooking up with a waitress. Well, now, you leave town. You don't call her. She thinks you're a jerk. You're going to come back to that club? Maybe not. I actually saw a guy hook up with two waitresses during the week and then for the weekend, they wouldn't work with each other. They were mad with each other because they thought they stole the guy from each other. That guy's not working that club anymore.

Don't screw the help. Hang out. Have fun. Have a good time. You really want to hook up with someone? Find an audience member. It's really easy to do. I've seen guys do it all of the time. Go to a coffee house, a bowling alley. Go to a weightlifting place. I go to the gym and work out. If you want to hook up with someone there, fine. But keep yourself occupied. That's really important.

Too many people on the road do drugs. They drink. It's a real easy and bad habit. They watch TV, the stupid talk shows all day. Go and do something productive. I know it sounds stupid but I go, I try to have a good breakfast. I work out during the day. And if I give myself a treat, I'll go see a movie. I'll go to the show, and I just feel better and I do some work during the day.

Don't get into really lazy habits of just watching TV and getting fat. It's a bad habit to get into. Keep yourself positive. Keep yourself upbeat. Do something productive every day. Have a plan. Go on the road and say, "Hey, I'm going to write a screenplay." Have a plan because if you failed the plan, the plan failed.

I spend a lot of time on the road, and if you're reading this book, you're seeing a prime example of how I followed a plan and kept myself busy. I worked out, took care of myself, and kept busy writing for my act, and putting this book together. And you can do the same thing. Maybe you won't be writing a book at first, but you can sure use the time to write material for yourself.

17

Showcasing With People

Let's say you live in Los Angeles or you live in New York, and you want to showcase for agents and managers. Here's what you need to do. Set up a showcase with people you trust and you respect. A showcase should last no more than an hour ten to an hour twenty. So you're probably going to need six or seven comics. Do not showcase more than 10 minutes of your set.

Too many people go, "I'm going to showcase a 20 minute set." Agents, managers, people in the industry don't need to see really more than seven. But if you want to do 10, fine, do 10. So get six or seven people, people you respect, people you trust, and people that are funny, and put together a show.

Comedy Career Management by Barry Neal

What you want to do is make sure that everyone is in charge of something. One person is in charge of faxing all the managers, calling all the managers, getting them to the show. One is doing agents. Maybe two are doing agents because there are so many agents. One is doing casting people. One person is in charge of making sure the audience knows from all the people because everyone has to bring people to a showcase. When you showcase, you have to bring your own audience because really no one is going to come to see just a general showcase of people they don't know. Each person is responsible for bringing 10 friends, 15 friends, whatever.

Make sure the showcase is in a good room, whether it's the Improv, the Laugh Factory, the Icehouse, or the Comedy Store. It's a good room. It's a good tape. It's a good setting. I got a lot of work out of doing a showcase at the Improv because again, we all worked together on it. We all brought a lot of people. We all made sure it was at the Improv. Everything was all set.

So again, make sure it's with people you trust and respect who are funny but they're different from you. Seven people on the show, no two should be alike. Also, do not set up a showcase with six people who stink to think you're going to shine. Doesn't work that way.

I've told you the story of the hack and the booker who said if he had known the hack was on, he wouldn't have come. It's the same principle. The showcase is as weak as its weakest link. So if you have six bad people, they're not going to say, "Wow, there was one great person and six bad ones." They're just going to say, "That showcase was a bunch of amateurs."

Seven strong people -- that's a good number right there, each doing 10 minutes. Bring in a guest M.C. If you can have a headliner, do it. I'm sure they'd be happy just to just to help you out, do some stage time and to M.C. a show. So have a good M.C., seven acts, all different, all strong, working together.

18

<u>Market Yourself</u>

After a show, you may want to market yourself with some product, something that says something about you. I sell T-shirts. I also sell CDs and my book. These are things that I do after the show, not only to market myself in terms of having people know who I am, but it's extra revenue.

It is amazing that people will come up after a show and want to buy these shirts or these CDs. Now people say, "Don't you think you're whoring yourself?" But you know, I don't know. All I know is bands do it. Ballplayers sell baseball cards. People have to promote themselves. And if *you* don't promote yourself, who will?

Now, first of all, it's really good extra money that I bring in on the selling of these t-shirts, books and CDs. But more importantly, I feel as though people when they wear it, they'll say, "Oh, we saw the Counselor of Love. He was great," or they'll listen to the CD. "This guy's great. You gotta listen to this guy. He's coming back in town."

I have the mailing lists. You can see those. What I do is I put those on the table. People fill out the little blank forms and I collect them. And after the show, when I'm done, I email people maybe two months before I get back in town, and I say, "Hey, I'm coming back. The Counselor of Love is coming back. You're on my emailing list." Or I send them a postcard saying, "Come on out. Come see the Counselor of Love." These are marketing tools that you really should start thinking about doing so you can market yourself. No one is going to work harder at marketing you than you. So put together some plans, whether you want to sell something, whether you want to do a mailing list, do something so people will begin to know your name.

Piece if advice -- if you are going to sell something, go either high end or go low end. If you want to sell something that's $15 like my t-shirts, that's great. Just bear in mind people aren't going to buy a lot of T-shirts because $15 is a lot of money. You can go the other route. You're going to sell something for $1. It'll probably cost you 10 cents to make. So you're making 90 cents on everyone, so maybe a bumper sticker because everyone has $1.

Funny story a comic actually said one time, "You know I'm not making that much at the club, so I'll sign napkins and everybody please give me $1." He did this! Forty people gave him $1. Now obviously you don't want to sign napkins, but he thought about it. He said, "I can sell anything for $1." So now he sells these cheap little things that you put a cup on and it just says his name. It costs him 10 cents to make. Everyone has $1. It's like a tip. So he gets like $40 or $50 extra every show. Well, you're doing seven shows a week, that's another $350. That's not bad for doing nothing.

So again, think about marketing yourself. Not only is it important in terms of creating more revenue, but it's important in terms of creating your name out there, getting name recognition and that's really what it's all about.

19

Traffic School

We've talked about how you have to be polite on the phone. Again, part of booking is dealing with bookers. Learn those phone skills. I can't emphasize that enough. When you get on the phone, learn how to say, "thank you", "please", "can I talk to him". Be nice to that person who's getting you to the booker. It's very important.

Now, what else can you do to start getting good at comedy? I think traffic school. Almost every town has it. It's called *comedy traffic school*. Now you have to get a license and you have to actually know the rules of the road, but what's great is you have a captive audience. I did it. A lot of comedians have done it. They do it for two or three years, and what they do is they learn how to deal with a captive audience, 20 or 30 people, and you teach them the rules of the road but then you have fun and it really helped me deal with the audience.

When I first started, I didn't know how to handle an audience, but then I did traffic school and I learned how to handle people talking to me, how to just interact with people, be quick on my feet. So think traffic school because you can also put jokes in.

I never stop my traffic schools. I'd like to try out five minutes of my material, because that's not what stand-up is. Stand-up is a dialogue where they don't know that you're just actually doing joke. You're just thinking of things that are funny, so the audience thinks. But I used to try material, weave it in and out of the day. And they never knew it was material. I'd just say, "Oh, you know, it was funny. Something happened yesterday." Well, it didn't, but they didn't know. They thought I was being honest. So you can actually try material out.

So go to your local comedy club and ask if they do a traffic school. If not, maybe you should start one. Start your own traffic school, a comedy traffic school. Believe me, it's a lot better than being taught by some cop who doesn't want to laugh all day long.

20

B. I. L. T.

I'm going to give you an acronym now and I know it actually isn't a word and doesn't really mean anything, but they're basically four words that can really help you in the long run. You may already have three of them, or you might even have four of them, and if you have all four, you're on the road.

B.I.L.T. B is for **brains**. You've got to be smart to do stand-up comedy, not only to market yourself, not only to deal with people, but you've got to be smart. Almost every great stand-up that I have talked to, and I'd say there have been between 50 to 100, are smart people. And I'm not saying necessarily college educated, although most of them are, but you need to have a good vocabulary. We communicate through our words, so you better pick up a book every now and then and read. And read the newspaper. If you're not smart and you

334

can't be self-reflexive, you're not going to be funny.

I is for the **internal fortitude**. You need to have that. You need to have what's inside and want it. You've got to be able to push through mountains. You've got to be able to say, "I know this is tough but I can make it" because there are going to be some valleys. There are going to be peaks, but there are also going to be valleys, and you've got to have the internal fortitude to say, "I can get through this." And people who don't have it, fall by the wayside. I've had students who have had 10 times the talent other students have had. They've had a lot more talent than I've had. They're not even doing comedy because they couldn't take the bad times. So know that in order to get good, you've got to go through the bad times. You've got to fail to succeed. You've got to risk to reward. So have that I, internal fortitude.

The L is for **looks**. And I hate to be shallow and talk about looks but quite frankly, if you're good looking and you're funny, you're going to be on TV because it's a great recipe. Take a look at the sitcoms. A lot of good-looking people, aren't there? Now you may say, "Well, what if I'm not that good looking?" There's nothing you can do about that, and believe me, I know. However, you don't have to be the best looking person in the world. If you're quirky-looking, or odd-looking, you have a different look, that's great. Know what your look is and utilize that. If you're quirky or odd, go with that. If you think you're dorky-looking, talk about that in your act. People need all different types on TV, especially for the secondary characters. So it's okay. If you have a different look, that's great. That's what we need. So the L is for looks.

The T is for **talent**. You gotta have talent. Talent of course is not the only arbiter but ultimately it will reach your ceiling. If you're not talented, you're just not going to be able to get as far as some other people. But I do believe this -- everybody has talent, at least some, and it's with hard work, focus and a plan that really will get you to almost to the top. Now there's that one or two percent, the geniuses, whether it's Jim Carey or Robin Williams, who obviously have just an incredible amount of talent. So again, all those things put together, you combine them and you have B.I.L.T. You gotta have brains. You gotta have the internal fortitude. You gotta have looks, and you've gotta have some talent.

Now believe me, I think of all those four, talent's probably the least important because you gotta have those first three. So those are the four things to really get you going. That's how to book a room. That's how to showcase a room. So we can get you out there because we want you to start making money. Stand-up is great. Stand-up is fun, but in order to make a living you gotta know how to book yourself. You gotta know how to market yourself and showcase yourself so you can start making your living and you can quit that 9 to 5 job and start having fun.

Conclusion

This is the end of Section number 5 and this is the last Section in this book. I want to thank you so much for taking your time and learning what you can about stand-up comedy. Stand-up comedy has been great for me. This is my life. This is what I love.

Now hopefully this book has taught you a lot. A lot of times books can only teach you so much because you gotta go out and do it and you may want to experience a class.

Well, I'm going to take a second to market myself. If you're interested, check out the website. I do teach, mostly just seminars now, and I do private consultations. So come check out the website. It's real easy. http://www.counselloroflove.com/. Come check out the website. If nothing else, say hello, say you enjoyed the book. Let me know how you're doing.

Anyway, I want to wish you all the best of luck. It's a long hard journey. But you know what? Keep in there. Keep the faith. It's a great journey. Enjoy the journey. It's fun. And when you get at the end you'll look back and you'll realize what a great time you had, so the best of luck.

ABOUT THE AUTHOR

Barry was born and raised in a suburb of Chicago called Lincolnwood, and attended Northwestern University, where he honed his comedy skills and ultimately became the Counselor of Love. After years of touring and headlining in many comedy shows, and becoming a regular at the famous Improve, he got his shot at the big time, appearing on the Tonight Show.

In his teens, Barry was the goaltender for the Midwest Champion Evanston Wildkats Hockey Team and played in Europe representing the United States. It was during this European experience that he learned to sing "Take Me Out to the Ballpark" in German. While attending Northwestern University, Barry performed with their IMPRO V troupe, the ME-OW show. Their director, Dan Patterson, Executive Producer of "Who's Line Is It Anyway," took the troupe to Scotland to perform in the Edinburgh Festival where the troupe had a successful run and received critical acclaim.

Comedy Career Management by Barry Neal

After college, Barry moved to Los Angeles where he began his professional stand-up career. After two years as a road comic in such hot spots like Moscow, Idaho and Lake Ontonagon, Michigan, Barry became a regular at THE IMPROV. He performed on numerous television shows including The Tonight Show, A&E'S An Evening at the Improv, MTV's Half Hour Comedy Hour, Fox Sports and Comedy Central's Short Attention Span Theatre.

Along the way, Barry began dating a beautiful princess he adored from afar during his college days. After a five year whirlwind romance, they made their living arrangement official by marrying in 1993. Happily married to his best friend, the nondescript Barry has become The Counselor of Love, sharing with his own humorous style the keys to a successful partnership.

Printed in the United States
71090LV00001B/15